MORE THAN Just a HAIRDRESSER

The ability to live a fulfilled and peaceful life **IS POSSIBLE** and completely within your grasp.

DONNA PIROMALLI

Donna Piromalli
Books & Coaching Programs

Books

More Than Just a Hairdresser - Book
More Than Just a Hairdresser - Workbook
The Art of Gratitude - Journal

Programs

THE ART OF LIVING PROGRAM
An individual program tailored to your specific needs for personal or professional growth or both.

THE ART OF POSITIVE CULTURE
An "in salon" program to address the needs of the business and group dymanics of the salon environment.

For More Information
Please Visit

www.DonnaPiromalli.com
www.griffithcounselling.com

Copyright © 2020 by Donna Piromalli

All rights reserved. This book may not be reproduced in whole or in part, by any means, without the written consent of the publisher. For permission requests, write to the publisher, addressed "Attention Permissions Coordinator" at the address below.

Donna Piromalli
P.O.BOX 1152
Griffith, NSW 2680
Australia

Acknowledgments

The number of people who have guided, inspired or accompanied me on my journey over the years are simply too many to name. These individuals include friends, family, coworkers, counsellors, educators, coaches, mediators and many others. Please know that I cherish the lessons learned and understanding gained through knowing each one of you.

Often you don't fully understand the influence someone can have on your life until you look back, years later. That is certainly true in my case, as I think through the time I have spent growing and learning to be the person and professional that I am today.

I can only hope that you all know how blessed I feel to have had you in my life whether that was for mere days or decades. There is no way to fully express my appreciation for the support and love you have shown.

I look forward to what lies ahead and anticipate an even greater understanding of all life has to offer. Thank you never feels like enough, but please know that I am so humbly grateful.

"The dream begins with a teacher who believes in you, who tugs and pushes and leads you to the next plateau, sometimes poking you with a sharp stick called 'truth.'"

— Dan Rather

Dedication

**I dedicate this book to my family.
To my husband Dom,
my 3 children Jenna, Anthony and Bianca
and my parents, Dino and Hilda Lucantonio.**

Thank you so much for all of your loving support over the years on my journey of both personal and professional growth. I treasure your warmth and caring and hope this book reflects the love we have shared. Without you, none of this would have been possible.

Contents

Introduction	9
Chapter 1: You are More than a Good Cut	15
Chapter 2: Therapist with Scissors	31
Chapter 3: Growth is Essential	45
Chapter 4: It's a People Business	65
Chapter 5: Design Your Own Path	85
Chapter 6: Make it Happen	107
Chapter 7: Work Smarter, Not Harder	121
Chapter 8: Connections	133
Chapter 9: Pulling Your Hair Out	147
Chapter 10: Living the Dream	163
About the Author	177

Introduction

You may find it hard to believe, but I dreamed of being a hairdresser for many years. While most young girls have a fleeting interest in working in the beauty industry at some point, mine stuck, and I was determined that would be my life. I started my career as a hairdresser at 16 years of age and loved it. It didn't matter to me that others thought of hairdressing as a job for those who couldn't do better. It was my dream, and I made it happen and grew that dream into a successful salon.

My name is Donna Piromalli, and I spent more than three decades honing my skills in the hairdressing and beauty industry. As I journeyed through life, I became acutely aware that I needed to learn more, be more and improve every area of my skillset to become even more successful. While I did that over time, it was an incredible struggle, and I learned many hard lessons about the beauty industry but also about myself.

When I thought about writing this book, I wanted something that would fill the gaps for those young hairdressers who, just like me, wanted success but were forced to trial and error their way along the path. So many very promising stylists eventually give up on their dreams as they become convinced that the struggle leads nowhere.

I am here to change that mindset. You can and will succeed if you have the tools to do so. Why wait and go through literally years of trial and error to learn the skills you need

Introduction

to create the life you dream about? It's so much easier to learn from someone who has been there, done that!

I also wanted to address the issues and concerns of salon owners. Having owned a salon at a young age, I made just about every mistake there was to make. I think most salon owners learn how to handle staff with ongoing difficulties to get along with one another to a certain extent. The main thing I learned through all that drama and turmoil is that no matter how bad things get, there are always solutions.

As I thought through the various events and lessons over the years, I realised almost every single bad experience came back to the lack of one skillset: Communication. Hairdressing is a very people-focused business. Unless you, as a stylist or salon owner, understand people intricately and have the ability to communicate well, you will never be free from the limitations holding you back right now.

Now, I am a professional counsellor, mediator and coach, and I help people navigate the issues they face in their business and personal lives, and this includes a large number of hairdressers just like you.

Within the pages of this book, I will discuss the everyday concerns you are probably facing right now. Only someone who has been in your shoes, as I have, can understand the daily stress of a salon and dealing with both clients and coworkers, not to mention family and friends. No matter what dreams you may have today, the path to success can be intimidating and frustrating as you seek to level up your life and your business but aren't getting anywhere fast.

I will lead you to uncover and rediscover those dreams you may have placed on the back burner and develop a plan to

Introduction

get there. The companion workbook that accompanies this book will be vital as you work step by step through what you want. This will allow you to clarify your path and set out on your own personal journey to success and happiness.

One of the hardest things we face as hairdressers is the fact that so many people make negative assumptions about beauty professionals. They have no idea the amount of training and intelligence it takes just to become qualified, and those negative opinions can easily make you feel "less than" or as if it's just a job.

We belong to a five billion dollar per year beauty industry, so it is vital to shift from the idea of a 'job' to a career. Once you embrace yourself as the professional you are, so will everyone else. As hairdressers, we are integral parts of our clients' lives, and a stylist is one of the few professionals that have the ability to affect the self-esteem and self-worth of those we serve.

We also often serve as our client's confidants. One of the more difficult things I experienced as a young hairdresser was learning to handle the sometimes confidential and intimate secrets that clients share. People tell things to hairdressers that they don't tell anyone else. This goes well beyond customer service, and we will talk about how those who learn to communicate with their clients while mentally protecting their own emotional energy are true winners.

As I grew as a hairdresser, one of my biggest goals was to become an instructor and take the stage with leaders in the beauty industry. In order to reach that goal, as well as other goals I had, I set myself on a path of lifelong learning that has never ceased.

Introduction

No matter where or when you start in this fabulous industry, only you determine where your own path will lead. It is empowering and a little frightening to think you have so much control over your destiny, but you do.

There is no question that the beauty industry is a very people-focused business, yet so few of us are taught to communicate effectively as part of our initial training. We are taught technical skills, which improve as we grow into our profession, of course, but if you don't pay attention to learning to communicate, your business will be stunted from the very start.

Understanding and developing emotional intelligence is the key to unlocking great communication and a prosperous future. This begins with understanding yourself, your client, your coworkers and your market.

We will discuss how to define success for yourself; not based on what others think you can do, or even what you think is probable right now — but on what is possible. We will explore the ideas of vision, purpose and goal setting.

The whole point of having a career is to create a happy, joyful life, but you must create that life for yourself. I will teach you how to manifest your future while paying the bills today. We all seek life balance, and learning to shift that balance as your business expands and personal life changes requires knowledge not only of what you want, but who you are.

As you move through the lessons I've laid out, you will understand that you can't wait for some picture-perfect life to start living. You have to begin in the chaos of now and change small things each day to find your joy. To accomplish

Introduction

this, I offer much practical advice for working with others and learning to have difficult, but productive, conversations that will clear the air rather than explode into conflict.

The whole idea behind this book is to shorten your learning curve and allow you to incorporate these things into your life quickly. This happens when you spend time imagining a new life and then forming and reforming a real plan – not a wish or a hope, but a step by step plan.

You can never underestimate the role of gratitude and how that plays into a peaceful, connected life. This is where the gratitude journal comes in. I'll teach you how to use this daily journal to be grateful for various things in your life, no matter your present circumstances. This includes learning to express that gratitude to those in your life in order to create a connection on an even deeper level.

Constant improvement requires both commitment and work ethic, but if you are willing to do the work, this book will take you farther than you can imagine right now. It will also make that journey much more enjoyable by teaching you to lower the ongoing stress in your life and lessen the drama.

I will warn you this is not one of those "Think happy, be happy" books. It is about creating a positive, authentic life that you can be proud of. This means incorporating a huge dose of personal integrity and learning to genuinely be the person you choose to be.

True happiness is all about loving the life you lead, and that includes excelling in your career. This profession can open the gateway to a life you never dreamed possible, as it did for me, and you can get to that dream much more quickly by purposefully choosing those who mentor you.

Years ago, I was taking a class, and a mentor of mine mentioned that I would be a good counsellor. I laughed it off, but he continued pointing out that hairdressers and counsellors share a lot of the same skill set. He was adamant that I was more than 'just a hairdresser," and he was right.

Now is the time for you to grasp the opportunity to move far along your own personal path. Just as my mentors showed me the way, I will show you. It's time you discover the incredible life that is waiting for you just down the road.

Chapter 1
You are More than a Good Cut

Chapter 1
You are More than a Good Cut

"So, what plans do you have for your career?" I asked a young hairdresser at a National Hair Expo in Sydney. I immediately received a deer-in-the-headlights glance as she paused. Crowds of hairdressers streamed down the aisle of the conference hall, splitting and converging around us like a huge river of humanity. I'd clearly caught her off guard. Laughter and conversations wafted through the air from all directions like a swarm of busy bees as I awaited her response.

"Um, what?"

"What are your career goals? Where do you see yourself in five years?"

She shrugged, "I don't know, having a job in a busy salon, I guess?"

There it was, the 'J' word, job. I could tell she'd never thought of hairdressing as a career. In truth, most don't - which is why I ask the question. Here we were at a national Hair Expo with some of the best hairdressers in the world, and it still hadn't occurred to her that she could be one of them. She could be up on that stage educating her colleagues from around the world just as they do, and just as I do.

Chapter 1

I will admit that few hairdressers start out on their journey with the thought that what they are doing is a career in every sense of the word. In fact, we've been conditioned by society to see hairdressing as just the opposite. It is often the butt of many jokes – that job you fall back on if you aren't smart enough to do something else.

In Australia alone, the beauty industry accounts for more than $5 billion in revenue each year. So, it seems a strange fact to know that so many of the professionals working in this incredible economic engine don't think of the industry as a real career.

Many years ago, while I was still in school and about sixteen years old, I recall having a particular teacher who used hairdressing as her example of failure. She'd say things like, "If you don't work harder on your next exam, you will end up being nothing but a hairdresser!" Or, "Students that don't turn in their assignments will be nothing more than hairdressers in ten years." Many people, even to this day, still see hairdressing this same way, as somehow 'less than' or as confirmation of some poor life choices.

Those of us who have spent decades in the beauty industry can tell you that it is anything but a dead-end job. We know the amount of training and education it takes to become a top hairdresser, and it's not easy. In addition to learning literally hundreds of techniques, one must also learn the chemistry of products, hair and scalp contagious and non-contagious diseases and disorders, as well as health and safety measures — not to mention basic business principles, management, marketing and entrepreneurship. Nothing about that is easy.

The idea of a 'job' versus career may seem like nothing more than being nitpicky, but it does matter. It matters because we all gain a great deal of self-worth based on what we do for a living. Think about how much time you spend working. It has a significant effect on how you view yourself and how you feel about your life. It then follows that if you internalise the idea that you are 'nothing but a hairdresser,' it lowers your opinion of yourself. It makes you feel as if nothing that you do for most of your time each day is worthwhile or valued.

There is absolutely no reason for that low opinion. Hairdressing is a valuable and needed skill in the marketplace and affords thousands of people a way to earn a great living and create a path toward business ownership. There are many individuals in other professions who never earn what we can as hairdressers and who never get the chance to own their own business.

I want you, and all those coming up in the industry today, to understand you have tremendous opportunities, so let the jokes and derogatory comments roll off your back. What other profession can provide happiness and improve the self-esteem of their clients? What you do makes a difference in the lives of your clients and will continue to.

You are Not Just a Hairdresser!

Your View of You Matters

Hairdressing is a skilled trade that can be used to build a wonderful and profitable business. While this often allows hairdressers to live better and have more opportunities than those who earn a traditional university degree, it's not a contest of you versus them or education versus trade skills. The real battle is you versus you.

Chapter 1

As a hairdresser, you provide a necessary and valuable service day in and day out. The beauty industry is all about helping people look their best and allowing them to feel confident no matter their circumstances. There are numerous career paths for those who are motivated to make hairdressing their true career and no excuse not to take advantage of those opportunities. That's not to say it's the easy path, it's not, but it is a valuable and profitable path.

As a young person, I was just as unsure of myself as anyone going through my training and then on to being qualified. Those first days and experiences are all new and fraught with uncertainty for us all. There is no way to avoid those early day jitters but to stride through doing the best you know how.

Will you nick someone's ear?

Did it!

Say something stupid?

Too many times to count!

Lop off half of someone's hair?

Yep, been there too!

The point is that every professional person starts out with those same uncertainties. A chef has to make that first meal for paying customers; a teacher has to face that first class; a surgeon has to cut into that first patient. It's no different. But how you view yourself does affect how you handle not only those first days but the days and years beyond.

As I said previously, I knew I wanted to be a hairdresser from a very early age. It was my dream job, and I wanted to be the best. It didn't matter to me what others thought because I had confidence and believed in what I was doing. I never saw my profession as 'less than,' but I met many hairdressers who did see it that way, unfortunately, and still do.

You have probably met some of them, too – those hairdressers who have no drive or motivation to improve. Those that hate coming in to work and perhaps don't treat their clients all that well. They are also the ones who complain about not having enough work or money. I'm here to tell you there is a direct connection between a bad attitude and a lack of success.

How you feel about yourself and what you do shows to your clients and affects your long-term success. No one wants an angry, unhappy, complaining person standing over them hacking away! I've met the shocked gaze in the mirror of a customer sitting in a chair while one of my colleagues told them how angry she was at her coworkers(chop) and her clients (chop, chop) and her husband (chop, chop, chop). The client's eyes grew larger with each snip of the scissors as hair showered onto the floor around the chair. I know for a fact that the client couldn't leave fast enough and never came back. Don't let this be you!

How you feel about what you do directly translates into who you are and how people see you even beyond the salon. This includes clients, colleagues, family and the general public. If you want to be taken seriously, then you must become that professional who views their occupation as a career. You train people how to treat you, and if you see yourself as 'less than,' so will they.

Chapter 1

You Choose Your Life

If only I had a dollar for every time someone told me they "fell into" hairdressing! No one lands here without making an active choice, most likely several active choices, which is true in every area of life. When someone offers this explanation, I dig deeper by asking questions and usually find they have a friend or family member who is a hairdresser and encouraged them to pursue it. They got the idea from someone or somewhere; it doesn't just happen.

For those who actively choose this path, it takes determination even to become qualified as a hairdresser and is much harder than most people imagine. If someone really 'fell into' the profession, it would be so very easy to quit along the way. By embracing the idea that this is a path you actively chose, it puts you in control over what happens next. What's important about that idea of choice is that you continue to choose. Do you grow, improve and change as you travel through your career? Or do you stay the same type of hairdresser with the same skillset as you were last year and the year before?

Either path is a choice, and it can be hard for some to understand that not choosing is also a choice — a choice to go backward. When I talk to hairdressers about their personal and professional growth, I am usually immediately bombarded with "I can't."

I can't take more classes because I have children.

Most of us have children and many are even single parents. If you want to improve, you will find a way as it also improves your children's lives as well as your own.

I can't spend any money because I'm not making enough money.

Growing as a professional and an individual takes an investment of time and money. The truth is that we never stay in the same place; we are either growing or falling behind. Which do you choose to be?

I am okay where I am. I have to live in the present, not the future.

While I'm a big fan of experiencing the present, the future comes at us quite quickly, and since there is no such thing as the status quo, you are choosing to be left behind and become more frustrated with the passage of time.

The point I'm making is that in a world of "I can't," be an "I can." You can change your circumstances just by learning from those around you. It is fully within your control to better yourself in one way or another, but you must actively seek that change.

When I was a young hairdresser, I had a colleague that had a booming clientele. I tend to be analytical, and so I mentally made a list of my qualities versus hers to try and understand why my business wasn't as bustling as hers. As I compared our technical skills, there was no doubt in my mind that I was a step above. In fact, I wondered several times as I saw the average cuts she'd done leaving the salon why her clients kept returning. But she had a booming business, so technical skill wasn't the deciding factor for these clients.

Every day I watched and listened as her various clients would come in. It baffled me for a while, but once I realised

Chapter 1

skill wasn't the biggest factor, I listened more closely to the conversations.

I am, by nature, somewhat reserved, so my gift of the gab was limited, especially in those early days. I had a harder time finding things to chat about to keep the conversation going as I was focused on the hair, rather than the person. I came to realise that this colleague did just the opposite. She focused on the person first, hair second. Some of her clients had been coming to her for years. She knew their children, their spouses, if they gardened or and where they spent their last holiday.

I distinctly remember this realisation as an 'ah-ha' moment in my career - when I discovered that this business is a people business, not just a hair business. If it was just about technical skill, then the most technically perfect hairdresser would have the biggest business. However, because it is people-focused, those with the ability to connect and engage their clients are the ones who really prosper, even if their skill is only average.

My discovery did not happen randomly. I chose to study and figure out why her business was so much better than mine. I discovered those things she did well, and then I chose to do something about it by incorporating some of those same communication skills into my own business. That lesson didn't cost me anything, and I will always be grateful to her even though she has no idea of the real impact it had on my career. The idea was something that I used to improve my whole business, and it was also a lesson in watching those who are successful to be able to replicate that success.

Be a Learner

The individuals who rise above and then move ahead in any profession tend to be those who choose to learn continuously. They put themselves in a position to learn from experts in the field and then work toward specific goals. They don't just sit back, content with 'good enough.' When you look at how people perform in any occupation, it looks like a Bell Curve.

On the first segment of the bell, you have the 20% of hairdressers that under perform, including about 3% that

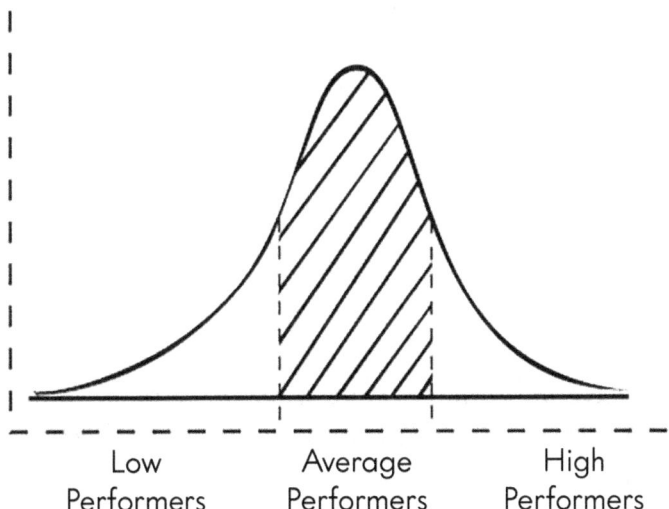

are the worst performers. That 3% might include the hairdressers who become qualified but never actually use their skills.

Now, you come to the large rounded portion of the bell. This large curve encompasses about 60% of all performers and is in the category we all lump together as 'average.' Not generally bad, but not great either.

Chapter 1

Then there is the last segment that includes the 20% that outperform all others. This includes about 3% who are the very top performers or experts in their field.

Now, think about this illustration for a moment. Where are you along that bell curve right now? Are you a young hairdresser who is just gaining skills, rising toward average? Or are you an experienced hairdresser who has acquired some good skills and wants to make the leap into that top 20% of performers?

No matter where you are on this curve, you can choose to improve. But it will not happen if you don't choose, and then do something about it. You can't just decide to do better, then not take any active steps forward.

Make the decision and take that first step.

And then another.

And another.

Make the commitment to be a life-long learner and add to both your technical skillset and the understanding of people as you go.

I want to point out that when I say a 'learner,' I mean to go beyond learning about hairdressing skills. While gaining more technical skills is always advantageous, remember that this is a people business first and a hair business second.

As my own experience has shown, you can have great skills and still not have a great business. This is because understanding people and learning to communicate effectively is the most important life skill you can ever learn.

Not only does communication affect your relationship with your clients, it also affects how you get on with your colleagues, your family and any other people who come into your life. Our entire existence is based on the relationships we have with those around us. How we communicate affects everything we do.

We will talk in detail about communication skills throughout this book because they are so vital. But commit right now to the idea that you must grow this soft skill set if you are ever to get beyond where you are right this minute.

Know Thyself

Have you ever heard the phrase, in order to understand others, you must first understand yourself? There is a great deal of truth to that. It is human nature to blame misunderstandings and poor communication on the 'difficult' people in your life. But take a look in the mirror. Are you really the difficult one?

No one wants to believe they are the bad guy, but I'm not talking about placing blame. I'm talking about taking personal responsibility for improving your life. That means, yes, there are difficult people, and at times we all can be that person. Even if we aren't the difficult one in a given situation, that doesn't alleviate our responsibility to improve communication.

One of the main ideas I'm going to present in this book is to understand those people and personalities that you have difficulty with and how to improve those relationships. In order to do that, you also must understand where your personal communication style fits and how you will need to

Chapter 1

alter that style with various types of people to communicate more effectively.

Because the hairdressing and beauty industry revolves around serving clients one-on-one, there can sometimes be a great deal of interpersonal drama. However, much of that could be reduced by understanding how to communicate better on every level. No one wants the stress of constant emotional upheaval and learning how to engage difficult clients and colleagues is essential. This includes being able to have hard conversations and make those constructive rather than destructive.

How many times have you avoided a conversation with a client or colleague because you knew it was going to cause drama? We have all been there! I once worked in a salon that had such a toxic interpersonal environment that I got physically ill every time I arrived at work. I allowed it to affect me for months just because I didn't want to confront the individuals or deal with the resulting drama! I was young and did not yet have the communication skills to set personal boundaries or address difficult topics, so I said nothing, and my health suffered.

As stressful as it is to have a difficult conversation, it can be even more stressful not to have one, and allow the problem to blow up into an all-out brawl somewhere down the road.

I believe so strongly in effective communication because I personally struggled with it for years. As a young salon owner, I took almost everything personally. If someone left my salon for another opportunity, I felt betrayed, as if they were disloyal to me. I didn't have the experience to understand it as a business decision on their part. Because of that, there were many people I didn't speak to again, and that was completely unnecessary. But, I didn't know any other way. I had not gained the skills to understand others and deal with difficult conversations in a professional manner.

That is the goal – to communicate like a seasoned professional. When drama is swirling around the salon, everyone feels powerless and productivity falls dramatically. Clients don't want to come to a salon that is always full of tension and drama, either. The truth is that you are not powerless, and once you have the skills to overcome personalities and difficult issues you move forward faster.

To do that, you must face some difficult and inconvenient truths about others and about yourself. I'm not saying this process will be easy; it won't be. But if you are ready to do the work, lower your stress and get better outcomes, then here we go!

Chapter 2

Therapist with Scissors

Chapter 2
Therapist with Scissors

There is no doubt that hairdressers perform a great service for their clients. We have the ability to make a client feel wonderful about themselves and leave the salon with a smile. Clients often become attached to their hairdressers for that reason, and communicating with that client can frequently veer into very personal areas. Of course, there will be a few clients who are also close friends, but for the majority of your clientele, you must constantly walk the line between professional distance and friendly confidant.

It all boils down to communication, and most of us start out with a great deal of anxiety about communicating with virtual strangers. I'm no exception. I remember watching experienced hairdressers keep up a near-constant stream of chatter whilst still performing with great technical skill. In the early days, if I had to talk to someone I didn't know, it took a lot of effort, especially when I was trying my best to do a good job. Like everything, once you do it awhile, it gets much easier. However, that doesn't relieve that initial anxiety with a new client, nor does it guarantee you won't say something wrong on occasion and risk ruining a client relationship.

Chapter 2

It is good business to be able to communicate well, but to do so and still retain those clients and coworkers, those communication skills must constantly improve. I am the first to admit that saying you must improve and doing so are very different things. Before you even start, you must embrace the idea that it is a journey, not a destination. Each step takes you further, but there is no such thing as perfection.

Taking a few steps forward and then falling back into old habits can be common. But it's not the end of the world. Communication takes practice, and you will get better as you continue to try. With that in mind, you must focus and plan toward improvement in order to make it a reality, and then continue with that goal of improvement in each situation — even if you are not perfect.

As most hairdressers quickly discover, sometimes you have to navigate awkward client situations that you have no idea how to handle at first. You have to not only be prepared to hear intimate and sometimes shocking details of a client's life without reacting, you must also know how to process that information and what to do with it for your own mental health.

There have been many times that a client has sat in my chair in tears. While I'm cutting their hair, they share how their husband is cheating on them, or how they have just been diagnosed with cancer. There is something about the element of physical touch that removes some of those normal emotional barriers we all have during our normal daily interactions. It makes the clients vulnerable, and so hairdressers often find themselves in a tough situation of wondering what to say, or more importantly, what not to say.

Therapist with Scissors

Sometimes it also offers an opportunity for comfort, not only for the client but the hairdresser as well. A hairdresser friend of mine had a client who lost a family member to suicide. The client was near inconsolable but needed her hair done for the funeral. My friend offered to have her come in well before the salon was open so she could be undisturbed and not have to face other people while being so upset.

My friend had also lost a family member to suicide and was able to sit and cry with her client. There are times we all step out of the professional role and step into the role of being human. Even when you don't know what to say, sometimes the mere act of listening helps. Times such as these are emotionally draining but very valuable to all of us.

Still, there are those times when 'awkward' can't describe what is happening with clients. Even after years, when you think you have heard it all, you haven't. I had a long-time client who found out her husband was cheating on her. It was a sad situation, and I realised that the woman he was seeing was actually another client of mine. I said nothing to either of them but made sure their bookings were on different days. Of course, the wife eventually discovered that I did both of their hair. She insisted I fire the mistress and only do her hair.

It was quite a scene, as you might guess, but those kinds of things come up frequently, especially in a small town. Preparing to manage those conflicts ahead of time leads to good outcomes, and honestly, what choice do we have? They will happen, and if you don't prepare, you have to deal with the sometimes disastrous fallout.

Chapter 2

A quick word here about coworkers: Those you spend most of your time with will inevitably affect your life, either for the positive or for the negative. We all spend the majority of our waking hours with coworkers — even more so than friends or family. The fact that you spend so much time together might lead you to believe that those relationships will be easier. I'm here to tell you they will not be easy at all.

In fact, the more familiar we become with someone, the fewer filters we use, so the more likely it is you will experience conflict with coworkers. I have seen many friendships, and even families, torn apart by the drama between coworkers in the same salon. That drama is very often the result of misunderstandings, bad communication and an inability to have hard conversations that are constructive rather than destructive.

As I pondered the true message and core of this book, I realised that everything hinges on the ability to communicate — with clients, coworkers, family and friends. If you learn nothing from these pages save the ability to understand and be understood, then I will have been successful. Everything in your life stems from your ability to communicate, and many of the problems or issues you are facing right now come back to this one skill set.

The Cast of Characters

I am sure you have seen or heard about personality tests. They are everywhere these days, but the tests have been around for years. The reason for that is that personality tests allow us to group people in broad categories based on their behaviors. This is handy because once you know the basic parameters of a person's personality, you can deduce the best way to communicate with them. This saves a great deal of trial and error, which can be disastrous for your business and stressful for you.

While there are many types of personality tests, and some break personalities down into numerous very specific types, I am going to keep it simple and talk about the four major types. Everyone generally falls within those four, for the most part. That doesn't mean someone is stuck with a specific type. Far from it.

All of us are a mix of these four types, but most of us have one dominant type. As we age, we naturally soften or mellow, picking up some of the positive traits from other personalities.

For example, when I was younger, I was not very outgoing or chatty. Over time, I watched and learned those outgoing traits from others and incorporated them successfully into my personality. We all do this on an unconscious level to a certain degree, but we can also speed up this process by focusing on areas within our natural communication style that we want to improve upon.

There have been personality theories that date back to ancient times. Generally speaking, there are four main types. Other models— such as the Myers-Briggs model, which has sixteen types— are still based on the four main types. For simplicity's sake, I won't go through all the various theories, but I will give you a broad overview of each type.

To set the scene for our discussion of communication and conflict resolution, we are going to talk about the four personality types as if they are your coworkers. They, of

Chapter 2

course, can also be clients or any other individuals you deal with in your life, but just for ease of discussion, they will be coworkers.

We can imagine a fictional salon that is busy and contains the following four hairdressers:

DeeAnn Dominant

DeeAnn is confident and is an expert on pretty much everything. She is unafraid to take charge and make things happen. She is a natural leader and is results-oriented. Many salon owners have her same personality.

People with DeeAnn's personality tend to be leaders, managers and CEOs. They can inspire and get people to go along with their plans quite easily. Many salon owners have these traits, and it helps make them successful.

On the downside, this personality can also be intimidating, controlling and domineering. They can treat others as less intelligent, and this personality may even come across as a bully.

Nancy Nitpicky

Nancy wants to get things right. She is focused and organised, and while she can be a bit of a perfectionist, you can rest assured she will tick every box and keep things running efficiently. Often accused of being anal retentive, she keeps meticulous records on every client, and they love how conscientious she is.

Those who are like Nancy also tend to be CEOS or senior managers but gravitate toward professions that are more meticulous, like finance, accounting or IT. Quite a number of hairdressers fall in this category due to the chemistry and meticulous nature of the technical skills required.

If backed into a corner, this personality can become a complainer or very negative, pointing out everyone else's deficiencies. While Nancy Nitpicky shares some of the same traits as DeeAnn Dominant, she tends to be more passive-aggressive when upset.

Sally Social

Sally can talk to a brick wall and enjoy the conversation. She is very empathetic toward her clients, and they trust her completely. She is often the one to rally those that are feeling down with her natural cheerleader spirit. Sally can be highly emotional and tends to be overly positive.

Individuals with this same personality will often be in sales. Many Real Estate Agents are classic Sally Social, and that's just one example. Hairdressers with these traits tend to have a huge following due in large part to their outgoing and fun personalities.

Some of the issues of this engaging personality are that Sally Social is sometimes not taken seriously. Because they are so fun, people tend to ignore this person's needs, and this can create a lot of drama. In fact, this personality is often labeled a 'drama queen' just because they talk about everything and everybody.

Patty Passive

Patty is extremely loyal and doesn't want to rock the boat. She goes along and gets along unless really provoked. Patty

Chapter 2

will put up with a lot from clients and coworkers and hates conflict. Her clients love that she is a great listener and keeper of secrets.

People who have this type of personality generally take jobs where they are in the background, like IT or writing. They love being in an active salon and are great team players, but not really into being the center of attention.

This personality will put up with a lot, but when they are done, it bubbles to the surface as a big blow up. They can also be passive-aggressive and can stir the pot from behind the scenes very easily.

I'm sure you recognise many people that fit into these four broad categories — in fact, we all do. But you should also know that most of us are a mix of these four types, and very few people have all the positives or all the negatives of any one type. Let me stress here that there is no wrong or right, better or worse when it comes to a personality type. They each have their specific strengths and they each have weaknesses — and every person contains part of all four personalities to varying degrees.

DeeAnn and Nancy both have powerful personalities and tend to be task-oriented. Sally and Patty are more emotional, but they tend to have much deeper connections with their clients. No matter which coworkers you put together in a salon, there will be conflict. Understanding these personality traits allows you to deal with them effectively and bring more overall harmony to your workplace.

While we all have parts of every personality within us, we are mostly one type. Age is a factor, as younger people tend to be more extreme in their personality type. However, time will allow them to absorb the other types so they can access those good qualities when needed.

Managing Conflict

The knowledge of these various personalities may not seem all that important, and in a perfect world on a perfect day when everyone gets along famously, it's not. But that isn't the world we live in. The world we live in is full of stress, conflict and misunderstandings.

What happens when an angry client marches into the salon and starts yelling at you? Or what about that client that says everything is fine, but then tells everyone that you are the worst hairdresser they have ever been to? And what about that coworker who is giving you the cold shoulder, but you can't figure out why, and now your clients are uncomfortable due to the tension?

These are the types of things that go on every day, and if you can't deal with them, or manage them to create a positive outcome, your life will be a wad of unnecessary stress. And who has time for that?

I talk to hairdressers from all over the world and at all stages in their careers. When I ask them what they need most, they almost never say, "I need to manage conflict better." What they do say, almost without exception, is, "I need less stress in my life!" Guess what? It's the same thing!

Reducing stress is all about identifying what is causing that stress, and then managing it effectively. Notice, I didn't say getting rid of the stress. There is no way to remove all the

Chapter 2

stress in your life. Even if you could, the minute you step into the workplace the next day, there's more stress. The real solution is in managing, not the elimination of stress.

Now think about the things that cause you the most stress from day to day. How many of those things involve other people? Almost all of them, I would guess.

Stress comes from feeling overwhelmed, frustrated and unable to live up to expectations. You have expectations from family, friends, clients and even coworkers. Everyone seems to have an opinion about how you live your life or how your career is progressing. Those expectations can be positive or negative, or both!

You absolutely can't control others, but you can influence how they see you by communicating better. While many expectations come from others in your life, they can also come from you. Feeling anxious or like a failure is often the result of not meeting your expectations, and that can be quite difficult to overcome.

To live your best life and continue to enjoy your career, you must learn the techniques to manage the conflict around you and within you. You can't be productive if all you think about is the conflict swirling through your life. How many times have you spent a day, or even several days, worried about an argument at home or a disagreement in the salon? How productive were you during those times? Not very, probably. That kind of stress directly affects your earning potential. When you aren't earning what you feel you should, what happens? More stress!

Remember, I said that the goal isn't to eliminate stress or conflict but to learn to manage it. You will always have those individuals that you have an extremely hard time getting along with. We all do. But you can still communicate with that person and be productive, and that is what I'm here to teach you: how to deal with difficult people – and how NOT to be the difficult person other people have to deal with.

Stress will always be present in your life to a degree. But your ability to manage that stress determines your overall long-term success, not only financially but in all the other ways that make life great. Your health, for example.

People deal with stress in many ways, and that can also include unhealthy coping mechanisms. Some smoke, drink, party or even overeat to escape the stress in their lives. None of those things help, because you get up the next day and the stress is still there. Only now you also beat yourself up for the way in which you cope.

It is very easy to feel like your life is spinning out of control, but you have much more power to affect the course of events than you may feel at times. When you try to juggle family, work, finances and the overwhelming feeling that you aren't measuring up, it's understandable that you want to run away from your life on occasion.

You feel like a circus performer trying to keep all the balls in the air and wondering when it will come crashing down. I have felt that when I drive along either to work or home, and the thought crosses my mind that I can keep driving, change my name and leave everything behind. That is not the answer, of course, but we have all had that idea cross our mind at some point, just because the stress of the moment seems almost unbearable.

While you can't always immediately change your circumstances, true power comes from being proactive and learning new, positive techniques to enhance your life. That will bring about the change you need to be happier and more productive.

There is a great deal of truth to the statement, "If you want to change the world, change yourself." That is because life is all about perspective. How you feel about your life affects how you view it. To make positive changes, you must first work on yourself.

We will talk more about the personalities, specifically how to deal with others in your life, in later chapters, but first, we have to talk about you. It's time to make some decisions, set some goals and step boldly toward that life you dream about.

Chapter 3

Growth is Essential

Chapter 3
Growth is Essential

Yes, I'd love for your business to grow, but right now, I'm not talking about the growth of your business. I also mean your personal growth. We all grow and change in some ways as we move through our careers and our lives, but that doesn't always lead to a better life or improve our growth as individuals.

When most of us first start out learning the industry, we generally work for someone else. Every new hairdresser has a lot to learn, and you have to get that experience with techniques and clients. Inevitably, you start to see things that can be improved. This may be in the way the salon is run, the way clients are treated or even something as simple as the more efficient ordering of supplies. The people you work with and meet open your eyes to opportunities and possibilities.

There is also a desire for improvement within each of us. When I was a young hairdresser, I wanted to be the queen of upstyles. It was a goal of mine, and I worked hard to achieve that goal. I also wanted to own my own salon. That is a huge goal for anyone, but even though I was young, I wasn't scared. I'd wanted to be a hairdresser my entire life,

Chapter 3

so even though I was still young, I wasn't put off because I'd thought about and dreamed of it for years.

Even as a young child, I would cut and style my dolls' hair until they were basically left bald! I played 'salon' for hours on end. Even at this early stage, I was fascinated with hair and how to help make people feel beautiful. My parents encouraged my interest. They would buy me more dolls, and I'd be off styling again. There are very few people who have such a connection with something at a very young age and then are lucky enough to make it their profession.

Those goals were very career-focused, and many of us have these sorts of big goals at various times in our careers. Even if you don't want to own your own salon, you do want to work in one that is innovative in terms of technique and marketing to attract new clients.

However, I had no idea in those early stages how important it would be to grow as a person. We all know that in this industry, no one is an island, and every day you must work with a whole variety of coworkers and clients. This can set up many opportunities for discord and stress throughout each day.

There is an old saying attributed to Ann Landers, who was Dear Abby: "Don't accept your dog's admiration as proof you are a wonderful person."

There is a great deal of truth in what she says. We are all the heroes in our own stories, so when things don't go our way, or we don't get our desired outcomes, we tend to point the blame toward others or the universe or whatever we feel might have caused the issue. Anything other than ourselves, that is.

Growth is Essential

To start on your path toward improving your life and reaching some fabulous goals, there must be a time when you have a really honest look at yourself. As we discussed in the last chapter, everyone has certain personality tendencies, some of which are positive, and some are negative. I've included a test in the workbook that you can take to see your traits. We each have a perception of the kind of person we are, but that is rarely the reality. Don't assume, use the data.

No person is able to see themselves in a truly objective fashion. But to move forward, you need to understand your personal strengths as well as your weaknesses. Once you see what those are, it is important to both accept them and work toward something better.

I'm sure you have heard the idea that to improve, you must own the parts of yourself that aren't exactly perfect. None of us are perfect, but the people who chose never to accept their flaws also never improve.

Let's look at an example. Let's say you take the test and find out you are a DeeAnn Dominant. Okay, there's a lot of good in that. Many CEOs and salon owners have that same personality. They tend to be quite goal-oriented and generally accomplish a lot. Now turn to the page that shows some of the negative traits of this personality type. How many of these do you recognise?

Really think about those. Do you sometimes talk over people or dominate conversations? Do you have a temper or negatively react when there's a problem? Can you be condescending or offensive to others? You must look at yourself honestly and think back to when conflicts have occurred in the past. How did you react? What was the outcome?

Chapter 3

One of the most important parts of growth is to evaluate yourself honestly. It is only then that in times of stress or conflict, you can stop and choose differently. Perhaps you stop yourself from becoming angry or think of why you are reacting the way you are and choose to change. Only with that understanding of yourself can you then plan to improve.

After all, the whole idea is to get what you want, right? You can't do that if you can't control your own emotions and understand where others are coming from.

The Power of Your Mind

Few people grasp how powerful the mind is. We take it for granted and don't realise how much of our life is controlled by how we have conditioned our minds – even without intending to.

Our minds naturally try to make life easier for us and use past experience to predict how things will go. For example, if you hop on a bike, do you have to think about how to push the pedals to make it go? No, you've learned in the past how to ride and balance a bike, and your mind has stored away that experience. Now, when you hop on a bike, your mind goes to that past experience and pulls out the instructions of how to ride a bike without you consciously thinking about it – no matter how long it's been.

Another example might be driving to work. How many times have you driven to work or back home, but not even remembered the drive? Your mind is helping you by putting that drive on autopilot. Now think about a time when you moved or got a new job. Did you ever find yourself outside your old place and not even remember driving there? Your mind has not yet been conditioned to the new location and instinctively takes you back to what it knows as 'home.' It can feel strange, but it happens to everyone.

Your mind uses past experience to predict what you need in each situation. You can think of it like a huge mental autocorrect. It tries to predict what you need and when you need it. This is very helpful because it frees our minds up to focus on other things.

While this function can certainly be very helpful, it can also hold us back when we want to make changes in our lives. You have to work to overcome those old mental habits to reteach your mind what direction you now want to go.

For example, think about someone you know who is always negative. They complain, gossip, nothing is ever right and all they want to do is talk about what is wrong with people or the world around them. That is a bad mental habit. It doesn't make them a bad person; they have just created a mental habit of constant complaining. Can they change it? Yes, of course they can! But it is a lot of work because that mental habit is so ingrained.

To understand why this is, it is important to know that the mind is made up of two different areas and how they function together. These areas are the subconscious mind, which involves about 80% of the mind, and the conscious mind, which involves 20%.

The subconscious mind is the emotional mind. It is our 'gut' feeling (intuition) and emotional reactions. It is our basic bodily functions, such as breathing, and our survival instincts. You can also imagine it as a huge library that stores all your past experiences, fears and set patterns of thinking.

Chapter 3

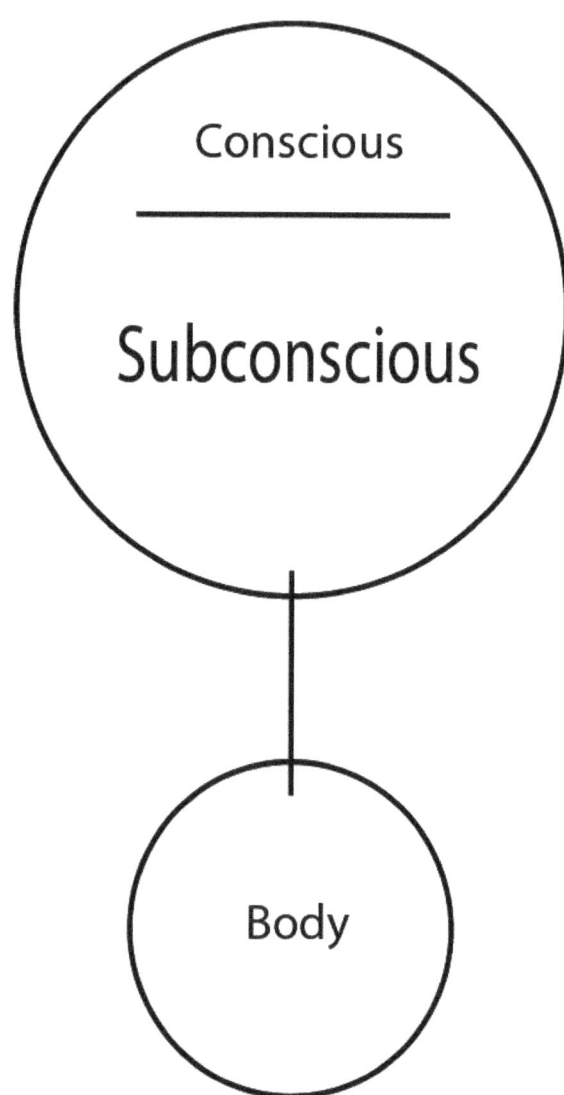

The conscious mind is where we learn. It's how we experience the world around us each day. The conscious mind is also where our logic and reason reside. It allows us to take in the world through our five senses and reason through what we experience. Those experiences or events are stored, and those become part of the subconscious mind. The conscious, or intellectual mind is what allows us to change our habits and ingrained mindsets. We are able to consciously focus on new habits until the old ones are replaced, which gives us a great deal of power over our lives and our futures.

This is great news! It means that nothing in your past controls you unless you allow it. You can do and be anything, but you have to make a decision first, and then take action to create a new habit. But if that is so, then why is it so hard to change?

The Battle of the Brains

It is weird to think that you have to battle your mind to create a new life or to set new goals. But it's true. We all have a lot of past experiences, both good and bad. We view the entire world through a lens colored by these experiences. This means we don't necessarily see the world as it really is but through our individual perceptions. We each have a slightly different version of reality.

You can see how stark this can be if you've ever had an automobile accident and read the statements of all the witnesses. They can be so wildly different; you have to ask yourself if you were even in the same accident! It is not that any one person is lying or misremembers; it is the fact that they each have a different perception of the events. They are not wrong, but none of them are all correct either.

This is true of all life experiences. You can even see it in your own family. How many times have you and your family members, especially siblings, talked about a past event when you were children and had completely different versions of what happened? It is very common because we all have this same perception bias. The trick is to learn how to compensate for that bias so that you have a more objective idea of what is or is not possible for your life.

Chapter 3

This is an important concept to grasp as you evaluate yourself. You must understand that even the idea of who you are as a person is different for everyone in your life because they view you through their own perception. You have this same perception bias of others as well.

When you try to change from an expected way of reacting to a situation or an expected pattern of belief about yourself, it's as if your mind fights for control. You have trained your mind to think a certain way, and it is working hard to 'help.' But now that you've decided to change something, it hasn't quite caught up to your new desires. That is why it's so easy to slip back into the old patterns and ways of being. Change is hard. Your mind makes it harder — at least at first.

Once you have focused on the new path and taken steps to create what you want, then your mind finally says, "Aha! I get where we're going now!" and helps you by removing some of those mental blocks. There are actually several set stages your mind and emotions travel through to achieve something - especially if it's something you've never tried.

I'll take you through an example to show how this works in real life. First, let's assume you've come up with a fabulous idea for your salon. This is an incredible goal with a lot of moving pieces. A great goal should scare you just a bit, and I know from experience that the idea of being responsible for an entire salon is a big, sometimes scary, goal.

This transition of thought isn't easy and takes work. One of the things I take my coaching clients through is illustrated in the chart on the next page. This chart visually illustrates the process of changing your direction and using your intuition to help your mind reset to a new direction.

Growth is Essential

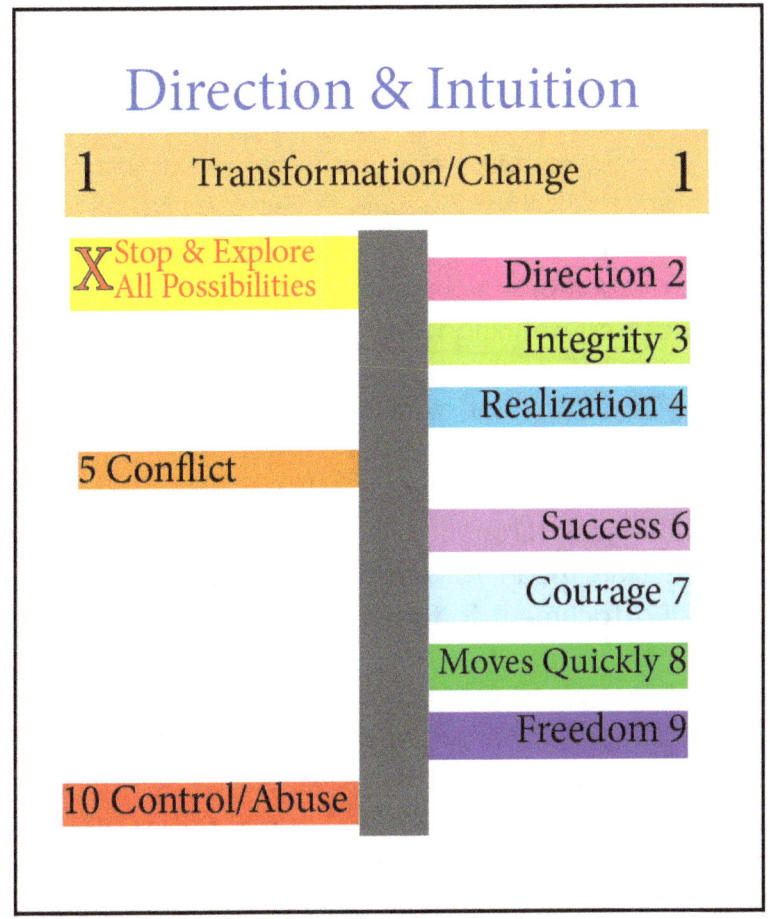

Now let's think about that goal. Imagine yourself at your salon. What does it look like? What is the name? How many people do you want working with you? What kind of clients do you want to specialise in? Think about it in detail. How will it feel to own your salon where you can implement your own ideas?

This is a conscious thought: a new idea — a new direction. You feel energised to explore all the possibilities and gain clarity on what it is you really want. You love this idea! You

Chapter 3

are thinking up innovations you want to try, and the creative juices are flowing through your intellectual mind.

Now you choose to sit with the idea a while. You explore the 'how' and possible steps you might need to take. This is where you think through and develop a more thorough understanding of what is involved. This solidifies your resolve to accomplish your goal. You are investigating the possibilities and defining ideas into possibilities.

It is very important not to charge ahead until you've had some private time to explore your thoughts fully. This is where 'gut' feeling, or intuition, comes in. Big goals take big belief, and as you work through a more detailed understanding of what it will mean to achieve your goal, you form an emotional attachment to the idea.

Now it's time to share the idea with others. This is one of the most dangerous stages where conflict often emerges. It is not uncommon to have a big dream shot down by those you love the most. This usually isn't because they don't want you to succeed. They are projecting their own fears on you and don't want you to fail. But that doesn't mean they are right. You may feel sad or overwhelmed at this stage as problems you didn't think of are presented and have to be worked through.

It is quite common for people to give up at this stage. It is just so much easier to go with the flow and live in that little box of expectations that others have for you. But that will not get you a better life. In fact, it will leave you angry, frustrated and resenting those you love. Don't fall into this trap. If you really believe in a dream, you owe it to yourself, and to those in your life, to give it all you have – they just don't realise it yet.

Growth is Essential

Once you have stepped back and worked through some of the issues that arose during this initial conflict stage, you can move forward. It is so unfortunate that many people never make it past this stage. They allow others to convince them they can't do it; that they can't achieve anything. Unfortunately, when you give up on a dream, it also becomes part of your past experience, and you feel like a failure from that point forward.

In truth, you didn't fail at anything; you just stopped moving ahead. But now, whenever the idea of owning your salon comes up again, you experience that sad emotion of failure, and it becomes even harder. For that reason, it is vital to work through this stage and realise it is just a stage. Every problem has a solution as long as you are willing to find it and keep going.

The next step is sometimes the longest as you put various aspects of your goal into action. But these initial steps prove your ideas and that you can succeed. You create courage from those early stages to keep going, but you have to have a plan. In the companion workbook, I will lead you though creating long-term and short-term goals.

Taking small actions each day toward your dream will allow you to achieve things much faster than trying to do everything all at once. It is okay to pace yourself, and planning is part of that pacing process.

One of the reasons I included a workbook with this book is that writing things down gets you one step closer to what you want. How many times have you come to the end of the year and realised you were in exactly the same place, with exactly the same problems, as last year? How many times have you set the exact same New Year's resolutions?

Chapter 3

Time gets away from us all, but if you plan, set goals and track your progress, you see exactly what you've accomplished. This gives you the push to accomplish more. If you never take the time to plan, you become a creature of habit. You live life on autopilot, never moving beyond where you are now.

Now, I'm not saying that all goals are easily reached. I can tell you they are not. When you try to accomplish big ideas, you will encounter big obstacles. But you are up to the challenge, even when it feels as if everything is slipping through your fingers and crashing around you.

I've had those days. I've spent a half-hour crying in the shower before work because things were a mess. Work was a mess, family was a mess, and I was a mess! We all have those moments. But that shouldn't stop you. It's a temporary emotion that passes.

Give yourself permission to feel discouraged on occasion, but know that discouragement will fade. This is where mentors or coaches can be of great help. Not because they make it easy, but because they have experienced those hard times as well and can help give you a balanced perspective. They can help you calm the emotional side of your mind and focus on solutions.

It is often during these very trying and stressful times when you want to move ahead, past issues and insecurities can arise seemingly out of the blue. Rather than see the situation objectively as just a tough obstacle to overcome, we start to internalise the discouragement.

This can present itself through negative self-talk as you start to think you are not smart enough, not good enough,

Growth is Essential

or not worthy of being successful. It's amazing how hard we are on ourselves for not being perfect.

There are also those who see you start to do better and become very jealous. They become an army of 'haters' attacking every imperfection or lack of progress. Some of these people can also be those you consider friends or colleagues. Though you may intellectually realise this comes from their insecurities, it is still very hard to deal with effectively.

This is when you must be ready to step into the next stage. When your emotions threaten to overwhelm or discourage you, go back to the facts. Go back to your plan, where you have written your goals and tracked accomplishments. Go back to where you are grounded. You will see that you have already come so far. You actively choose whether to get dragged into the old negativity or to break through it to something better.

None of those spiteful comments are really about you. They are about those who aren't achieving their own goals. Part of getting rid of an old way of thinking is also getting rid of the habits of backbiting and revenge. It doesn't serve the new you, so let it go. When they can't drag you back into old negative habits, you have won.

One of the hardest things to understand is that as you grow as a person and an entrepreneur, not everyone can make that journey with you. Those people must be left behind, not because you don't care for them or even love them, but because they allow their issues to stop their progress. Again, it has nothing to do with you, but the fact that you are moving ahead highlights the truth that they are not.

Chapter 3

There is much wisdom to the idea that what you focus on expands. If you focus on your positive life goals, that positivity will increase beyond what you can imagine. But if you focus on negative habits, they will move your life in the exact opposite direction. There is no such thing as stagnation because life isn't lived in a holding pattern. Everything changes, and you either move forward or backward. Your choice.

Once you decide to focus on the facts and ground yourself, your conscious mind will again help you. You will be able to concentrate on the task at hand and find solutions you weren't aware of previously because emotions were pushing out logic and reason. This is a great trick for anytime your emotions are getting the best of you. Focus on the facts of the situation and allow the conscious mind to come to your rescue.

Danger: The Spiral of Doubt

Fear is a terribly scary thing. It is what keeps so many from even setting goals in the first place. It's pretty sneaky, too. Once you get discouraged, those old negative thought patterns sneak right back in. It is very easy to feel the situation is hopeless. You may even question if you want that goal anymore because it seems so hard to achieve.

The main issue with this is that you no longer see issues objectively. Your mind has created this alternate story to save you from being judged by others or from failing. You become so fearful things won't work out that you start creating excuses for failure before it even happens. Unfortunately, these excuses become self-fulfilling and lead you right into the pit you were trying to avoid.

Doubts and unrealistic fears destroy inner clarity. These are often caused by outside influences making judgments about what you should or should not do. Have you ever sat with family or friends and had them discuss your decisions right in front of you as if you weren't even there? This has happened to me with my colleagues. They don't hold back either, discussing how stupid some decision was or how I should have seen this or that in advance. It's humiliating.

It's even worse when you hear it second hand. You feel as if your decisions are the hot topic of conversation around the water cooler!

All this outside chatter causes the situation to become even more muddled. There appears to be no satisfying solution and too many differing opinions. At this point, your mind begins to feel like a twisted ball of string desperately wanting to unravel itself. The more you attempt to control the situation and listen to and please outside influences, the more anxious you will become. Your doubts and fears of making the wrong decision become too stressful and confusing.

The only cure for this is to stop. Worry is stress over things that probably won't even happen. Stop allowing the 'what ifs' to stagnate your progress. Relax and let go of those thoughts. Do nothing for a bit, and allow things to work themselves out. You can't force things to happen. All you can do is point yourself in the right direction and make those little steps of progress. Allow the chatter to die down both internally and externally.

This is the time you need to be around those who cheer your progress and encourage you to keep going. It can be very easy to descend into self-sabotage when you feel as

Chapter 3

if you are in a void. Only you have the ability to recognise the turn your emotions are taking and put a halt to that thought process. Once you recognise it and redirect your thinking, things automatically improve. This is because those thoughts were all about emotion, not reality.

You are the exact same person on the bad day as you were on the good day. The only thing that has changed is your perception. That is driven by emotion. Go back to the facts, get grounded and move on.

Practice the Pause

Often, the difference between internalising negative emotions and grounding yourself to move forward is simply a thoughtful pause. When you hear something negative, a normal response is to react negatively. That starts the spiral of doubt.

Every single chart I use with my coaching clients starts with this type of pause. Explore all the possibilities as objectively as possible. This means taking a break from the thoughts swirling through your mind and actively look for solutions. Perhaps talk to a mentor or colleague who is doing what you want to do. Ask questions. It's odd to think asking questions is moving forward, but it is. You are doing something other than worrying or focusing on obstacles, and that is forward motion.

However, if you get in the habit of pausing before you react and think about the event or comment that just happened, you can step back and choose not to get pulled into that negativity. Your workbook has a circle of control illustration in Section 2 that shows how this works.

Rather than roll through the gamut of negative emotions, you simply choose to reject them and move on with what you are doing. You don't have to come back later to ground yourself in facts because you do it immediately.

While it takes practice, this can become an invaluable tool to expand the good things in your future. Rather than be on a constant emotional roller coaster manipulated by others, you are in control and determine what will or will not affect your emotions and your life.

Essentially, you are empowering yourself with the strength to walk away from things that don't serve you — like negative emotions. Will you be 100% successful? No. But you will eventually get better at it. The more you can leave those negative emotions on someone else's doorstep, the happier you will be — even if you haven't achieved one of your goals yet.

The whole idea of this book is for you to find your version of happiness and fulfillment. Taking back control and power over your mind and your emotions is one of the most important things you can do to achieve that happiness.

This one idea will allow you to have a happier, more productive life than a vast majority of the population.

Stop, Pause, Consider and then Move ON!

Chapter 4

It's a People Business

Chapter 4
It's a People Business

Anyone who has ever been associated with the beauty industry will tell you it is a people business. That is to say that the professionals in the industry have a direct impact on their clients' lives on an emotional level. How often have you given a client a great cut and style and they instantly smiled? They feel like a million dollars and walk out of your salon on cloud nine. Conversely, when a client is displeased with how they look, it is the exact opposite.

I have had the experience on occasion where a client's expectation was not fulfilled for one reason or another. Because beauty very much affects a person's self-esteem, it is not unusual for that disappointment to show in an emotional way. That client may angrily yell at you or burst into tears.

This is one reason that I learned to ask so many questions of a new client upfront. I learned that disappointing a client or allowing them to have unrealistic expectations in the beginning could be emotionally traumatising. Someone unfamiliar or new to the beauty world may not fully grasp this idea and will consequently have a much more difficult experience.

Chapter 4

Understanding people is the real key to unlocking a prosperous future. This begins with understanding yourself, your client, your coworkers and your market. All of these areas matter, and if you roll along in a reactive way, rather than learning how to manage various situations proactively, you are setting yourself up for a difficult and stressful road.

Emotional Intelligence

You have probably heard about the idea of Emotional Intelligence. It has been around in the business world for many years now, and the phrase was made popular through a series of books by Daniel Goleman. The whole concept of emotional intelligence is that we each have the ability to be aware of, control and express our emotions. This means we are able to handle interpersonal relationships with clear thought, understanding and empathy. In other words, we think about and choose how to react to people rather than doing so on impulse or reaction.

The ability to grow in the area of emotional intelligence means that you will be able to deal with all people much more efficiently to achieve better outcomes.

This may seem like a deep subject when all you want to do is improve your relationships with coworkers and with clients. But people aren't easy! We are all very complex beings, and to gloss over these ideas or make them seem easy is an incredible disservice to every single hairdresser, in my opinion. We have all spent years upon years with our profession being discredited as insignificant, but we all know beauty is vital to our client's wellbeing and how they feel about themselves.

It doesn't help that much of the beauty industry is female-focused and female-operated, either. It is as if that gives the whole world permission not to take it, or us, seriously. If we are to truly make a difference in our lives and our profession, we must take it seriously. That means we take these relationships we are creating seriously and work on our understanding of things such as emotional intelligence.

Goleman put forth that five main elements of emotional intelligence must be addressed in order to move forward.

They are:

- **Self-Awareness.**

- **Self-Regulation.**

- **Motivation.**

- **Empathy.**

- **Social Skills.**

We will talk about each of these areas separately, so that you can gain a much better understanding of the areas that are fully within your control to change.

In the previous chapter, we touched on the idea that the subconscious mind is very powerful. We discussed the fact that it controls fully 80% of your actions and emotions, while the conscious mind has only 20%. Let's go back to the following diagram that was first developed by Dr. Thurman Fleet almost 100 years ago.

Chapter 4

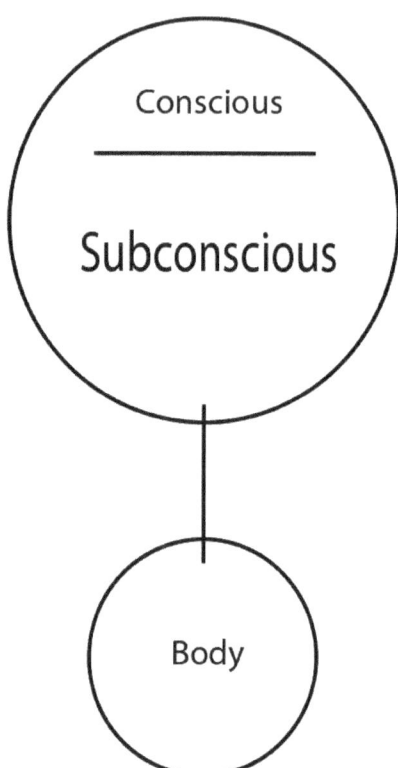

We will dig a little deeper into the meaning and workings of the mind on these levels so you can understand how they work and how you can use them. The conscious mind is the thinking mind that gives you the freewill to exhibit certain actions or behaviors. It receives your initial thoughts or impressions of situations and determines whether to accept or reject them.

For instance, I made a conscious decision to limit time watching the news, especially early in the day. This is due to the fact that the news tends to be so negative. I felt it was important to set a positive tone for each day. I thought that if I went in to deal with clients and was already worked up about something in the news, it would alter how I responded to everyone and everything.

It may seem like a small decision, and it was, but it made a big difference in how I mentally viewed each day. This is an important point. The changes in your life don't all have to be huge to have a big impact. Even small changes to the things you normally do add up and can significantly impact your life in unexpectedly positive ways.

The conscious or intellectual mind initiates your logical thoughts while the subconscious carries those ideas out. You can think of it like a gardener tending a garden. The conscious mind decides what seeds to plant in the garden, and those seeds are tended and grown by the subconscious mind. This is why it is so important to choose positive ideas and growth-oriented actions to focus on.

The subconscious mind doesn't know the difference between what's real and what's not. So, it will grow any seed you plant. If that seed is negative or one of self-doubt, then your subconscious will grow that seed, even if it harms you in the long run. Another interesting truth about the subconscious mind is that it is always working — even when you sleep!

If you plant feelings of inferiority and unworthiness, for example, those ideas continually circulate. This is why so many people feel emotional and depressed, but they can't figure out why. Those negative thoughts aren't being actively replaced, so they continue to feed on one another behind the scenes in the subconscious.

Part of achieving emotional intelligence is to understand that you have more power over your mind than you imagine. By purposefully focusing on the things that move you forward and taking action, you can leave that old mindset behind and live a more peaceful, productive life.

Chapter 4

The funny thing about the work you are doing on your thoughts is that your clients will be the first to notice. When you focus on filling your mind with positive thougts, your outlook naturally improves. You are happier, and it shows. Clients are drawn to happy hairdressers! Not the fake, pretend-happy, but the real authentic kind of joy that comes from your growth as a human being.

Many people want to divorce the ideas of business and personal life completely. They seem to think that once you step in the doorway, you can switch thoughts or emotions on and off. As hairdressers, we cannot do that entirely. What we do is intensely personal for our clients, and how we feel about ourselves personally has an impact on our professional lives. While you don't want to share all the parts of your life with clients, they can tell when you are happy or not. No one wants an unhappy person standing over them with a pair of scissors!

Stephen R. Covey, the author of The 7 Habits of Highly Effective People, stated it this way: "Our ultimate freedom is the right and power to decide how anybody or anything outside ourselves will affect us." This is where your conscious, or intellectual, mind needs to be exercised. It will help you to be in control of your mind, rather than letting the outside world control your emotions and actions.

Self-Awareness (Perception)

Self-awareness is the ability to step outside our thoughts and attempt to view ourselves objectively. How are we, really? What do we do well? What areas need work? Self-awareness is bundled tightly with perception. It is almost impossible for us to be completely objective about ourselves, especially at first. This is because we view everything, including ourselves, through the lens of perception.

Perception is the meaning you give to everything you experience. It is the lens we see through to understand life. I'm sure you have had the experience of people whose perception of life is very negative. If the sun shines, it's too hot; if the rain falls, it's too wet; if a bird sings, it shatters the peace.

None of these things are good or bad; they just are. We each experience them and then assign meaning based on our perception. While we don't think about our perception, it has a tremendous power to change how we experience life. It is the interpretation of events that determines our emotions, and our interpretation is based on past experiences. What we don't realise is that these prior experiences are altering how we perceive the present and think about the future.

Often these perceptions are developed in childhood and have nothing to do with today. A child may think they are not gifted or intelligent or beautiful because of some random comment in their youth from an adult. It has nothing to do with reality, but if you interpret that comment as truth and believe it, it can seriously impact your life as an adult.

Just as my instructors in high school used hairdressing as an example of failure, I could have easily believed that and assumed that, because I wanted to be a hairdresser, I was a failure as well. Thankfully, I did not believe those adults, but it easily could have happened.

This is where self-awareness comes into play. To take the first steps toward true emotional intelligence, you have to consciously think about your current perceptions and

Chapter 4

attitudes. Think about the very first time you had that perception. How old were you? Many people develop perceptions before the age of five or six and carry them for a lifetime.

Now ask yourself, what happened to give you that impression? Perhaps it was an overheard conversation or a comment written about you by a teacher or parent. Maybe even something that happened with your peers at a young age.

Now you have to decide, is it true today? Most people can definitively say that those long-ago perceptions are no longer true. This allows you to actively refuse to allow a negative idea to be part of your ongoing understanding of yourself.

We have become very different people over time but often still carry around some of those negative ideas formed in childhood. There is no reason for this except the fact that we haven't consciously chosen to reject those thoughts. Once we do, our perceptions shift for the better.

One word of caution here — this is an area where those who have known you for a long time can be very difficult. They may also still carry around the mistakes you made while young or perceptions they had of you years ago. Just because you decide to reject those ideas doesn't mean they will. You must be persistent in your thoughts. They may still bring up things you did as a child or teenager because, to them, you are still that person. Set that aside. You can do nothing but be different to change that perception. Just like Stephen Covey said, you have to commit not to let those outside ideas alter your new sense of self.

This is one area where the victim mentality can bite you hard. If you have had a difficult background, then the ideas formed about yourself during those troubling times can be tough to leave behind. But it's not impossible. It is a habit to make repetitive excuses if you've gone through a hard circumstance, but don't let yourself off the hook. The past is not the present, nor is it the future. While you can't change things that happened, you can change today, and you can improve tomorrow. Letting the past define who you are now, or what you will become, never has a positive outcome.

I know many young hairdressers who are also single mothers. I was as well. Some choose to let those circumstances define what they are or who they will be. I hear things like, "I have a kid, so I can't get more education," or, "I can't have my own salon. I have a kid to raise." We all have kids to raise! Having children does not determine your success or failure. You do.

The real problem is that they perceive themselves to have already failed and don't even try. But is that reality? NO! They haven't failed anything other than perhaps their own, or someone else's, expectation that wasn't realistic in the first place. They can still be successful, but the feeling of disappointment or failure has to be set aside first.

Self-Regulation (Will)

Every day, we test our ability to self-regulate. This means we decide to make a change or to do things in a certain way, and we either succeed or fail. It doesn't matter if it is trying to refuse a scrumptious piece of chocolate cake or not to hit the snooze button one more time in the morning. We have to decide between what we know we should do

Chapter 4

and what we want to do. The ability to resist temptation is commonly described as self-regulation or willpower. Our will is essentially a mental muscle, and certain physical and mental forces can weaken or strengthen our self-control.

I like to couple the idea of self-regulation with self-forgiveness. Not only is it important to work on self-control in regard to reaching goals, it is also important for our emotional well-being. The inability to control emotion can be devastating. Not only can it lead to blow-ups that completely ruin both business and personal relationships, it can also mean we continually beat ourselves up for tiny imperfections.

This is another area where the ability to take a pause and consciously consider our thoughts is so valuable. When you are beating yourself up for having that extra piece of cake or talking negatively about a client at the salon, stop. Stop and think about where that thought originated. Was it one incident or event in the past that made you feel like a failure? Probably so. Can you do anything about that now? No, it's in the past.

Now is the time to mentally forgive yourself and commit to strengthening your will. When the situation presents itself again, imagine handling it perfectly. Think about how you will walk away from the negative talk or refuse that delicious slice of cake. Think about how proud you will be when you accomplish that goal. Now hold on to that feeling. This is how your mental muscles grow. Through repetition in your mind, you train your subconscious to handle the situation. The next time you are presented with that same scenario, you will find it much easier to triumph because you are harnessing the power of your subconscious mind for help.

Motivation (Imagination)

Strengthening mental muscles also means actively trying to understand how your life can be different. Imagination is the ability to look at any situation from a different point of view (perception) and enables you to create a new reality that allows the possibility of change. If you have a negative perception and don't believe your life will ever be different, how can it be?

Albert Einstein once said, "Imagination is everything. It is the preview of life's coming attractions." You have to allow yourself to imagine that you can change something about yourself before that change can happen. If you never entertain the idea of that change, there is no hope that it will occur.

The fact is that you must convince yourself first, and then you convince everyone else. There is a quote attributed to Henry Ford that says, "Whether you think you can or you think you can't, you are absolutely right." You have tremendous power to change your own life, but only you can imagine that new life and bring it into being.

I have had people tell me that they couldn't do this. That they couldn't imagine a different life because it was 'not reality,' and they were 'realists.' I was speechless, which rarely happens. If you don't think change can happen, it can't. It's that simple. Being a 'realist' is nothing more than fear of change, and a refusal to consider life might be better than you think it is right now. This is very sad to me because to protect themselves, these 'realists' have completely closed the door on any chance at a better life — and they do so willingly.

Chapter 4

I understand that many people who refuse to imagine something different for their lives have many reasons for that mindset, even if they don't consciously realise it. They may have been told repeatedly as a child that they must accept their lot in life and to try better was to betray their upbringing. They may have been so traumatised by a previous failure that they believe not trying saves them from the pain or the embarrassment of failing again. They may fear change so much that they'd rather stay right where they are than do something different — even if the life they have now is unsatisfying or very difficult.

You must be able to imagine a different life in order to get there. No matter your age or circumstance, you can practice this skill and build it to the level that serves you. When you understand how to harness the power of your imagination, you are on the path to success and fulfillment.

Empathy (Connection)

Our lives are defined by memories utilised by both our conscious and subconscious mind. You may remember falling off your bicycle as a child, but do you remember every single time you fell? Probably not. That doesn't mean the memory is gone; it is just hidden in the vault of your subconscious.

As you learned earlier, the subconscious mind is the warehouse where all memories and experiences are stored. In fact, all information that comes to you through your senses is stored in your subconscious mind. Your conscious mind is what you use to retrieve the information that has been stored, and it is often very selective. However, just because you can't actively remember or pinpoint something, doesn't mean it can't affect you.

When we talk about empathy, we are defining it as the ability to understand life from another person's point of view. This is important because empathy is the cornerstone of trust, and the inability to trust others can have a tremendous impact on your personal and professional life.

As a hairdresser, creating a rapport with clients is essential. If you have your own trust issues due to things that have happened in your past, it will limit your ability to open up to people. That means they will be just as reserved with you, and that lack of trust will not create a strong relationship.

Often, we will have a 'feeling' about a person or relationship. Something feels 'off.' You can't put your finger on what it is, exactly, but something is preventing you from fully trusting that person. This is your subconscious, or intuition, at work.

You may call it a hunch, gut feeling or that little nagging voice, but it causes you to pause or hesitate. Each of us was born with a natural intuition, as it is a basic human survival instinct. As children, we all follow our intuition more naturally, but as we grow and age, our conscious mind encourages us to ignore intuition. This is because we often can't pinpoint the problem, so our logical mind tells us a problem doesn't exist or is no big deal.

However, our sense of empathy is greatly impacted by intuition and can be strengthened and cultivated. It involves being our authentic self and then determining if others are being authentic as well. As we become more sensitive and trust our natural intuition about people, we

Chapter 4

know immediately who we can trust, and they sense they can trust us as well.

Hairdressers are often told many personal details and family secrets. Being the kind of person who is trustworthy means being empathetic to your clients and how they would feel if you shared their personal details with the world. The same is true of your coworkers.

I think we have all been in the situation where someone shared something about a client or a coworker that was very uncomfortable. This is not just harmless gossip. The lack of empathy shown by a person who shares the secrets of others is very telling and can ruin a hairdresser's career, not to mention many personal relationships.

Social Skills

'Social skills' is a bit of a broad term, but it is essentially our ability to get along with all types of people. This is critical if you are to change your life, because it's not just about you. While you must change yourself first, you also have to change how you deal with others to reach the kind of life you dream of. We will spend a lot of time in the remainder of this book talking about the various personal and professional social skills you must have and how to improve them.

These skills include such things as:

- **Persuasion and Influence**

- **Effective Communication**

- **Conflict Management**

- **Leadership**

- **Building Rapport**

- **Collaboration and Teamwork**

In your workbook are several charts that illustrate how these ideas influence and are enhanced by one another. These include existing relationships, responses to conflict and a mind and thoughts chart. I think it helps many people to see this in visual form to understand.

I realise it sounds like a lot, but many of these skills cross over from one to another. Once you understand how to apply them to the basic personalities you encounter every day, your life will become easier, and outcomes will be much more predictable.

The beautiful thing about learning about each of these areas is that they apply both professionally and personally. I know many of us have had the experience of our professional life going well, while things at home seem like a disaster. And, conversely, when all is happy at home, the salon is a nightmare.

Part of the reason for this is that we aren't learning skills that can be applied in both areas to keep everything running smoothly.

The Gift of Reason

After reading this chapter, you may get the idea that humans are a mess! But we aren't. In fact, we are the only animals who can perceive our inadequacies and then do something about them. We can reason through situations

Chapter 4

and find a better way, and this ability to reason is something that grows with us.

As we age, we can look back and review parts of our lives — even particular past events. What we think about those events, or how we interpret them, changes over time. This is because we gain experience and can see ourselves much more objectively. We also gain empathy and have a much better understanding of why people act the way they did or make the choices that affect our lives.

Young children don't have the ability to choose for themselves the thoughts, beliefs or ideas they will adopt. They accept everything as truth. This is something we can only understand about ourselves as we age and look back at our lives. We realise some of the ideas we accepted as fact weren't our ideas at all but simply the statements of those we trusted.

Until a child reaches about eight years of age, everything that the child learns and experiences ultimately becomes their self-image. This explains so much about how we are today, but it also allows us to reject old ideas and actively change that prior perception to something new.

Many people never take the time or energy to engage in self-reflection and live their lives on autopilot. They react as they always have, hold tight to beliefs and ideas they have always had, and never question or think about a different life. You will often hear them say, "Well, that's just the way I am. Take it, or leave it."

We each choose every day how we will be; nothing is set in stone. There is never a case where you 'are the way you are.' You are the way you choose to be right now, and you make that choice every day.

You may already know intuitively that your life can be different; you only have to decide to make it so. It will be work, but I believe that a peaceful, productive life is worth that work.

It is a wonderful thing to know our past is not our future. It opens the door to infinite possibilities, but only you can choose to walk confidently through that door.

Chapter 5

Design Your Own Path

Chapter 5
Design Your Own Path

Over the last few chapters, we've talked about the issues we all face, both in our professional and personal lives. You know things can be different, and now we are going to dig into the nuts and bolts of how you make those changes.

First, you must make a series of decisions. These are the decisions that will give you a framework. The wonderful part of this is that you decide what that framework will be. Not me, not your family, not your colleagues. No matter what anyone else thinks you should do with the rest of your life, you are the ultimate decision maker.

Most people don't spend time actively thinking about how the rest of their life is going to play out. They may set the occasional goal, such as to lose 5 kg or attend a national conference, but they don't have a vision of where their life is headed.

Stopping your busy life and making time to set goals, think through issues and then revisit those ideas regularly may seem like a lot of time to invest in thinking. I've even had

Chapter 5

some very pessimistic individuals say it's nothing more than daydreaming. I strongly disagree.

If you have no endpoint in mind, how do you ever achieve great things? Do you start a trip having no idea where you want to go or what you want to experience? I think not. But not having a plan is one of the main reasons I feel so many people float through life on autopilot. Every day, month and year largely remain the same because they haven't designed their life as a series of stepping stones to reach a goal. Instead, they roll with what life presents, and nothing changes much.

An illustration that shows the difference between these two mindsets is to imagine two people who say they want to run a marathon. One sits down regularly and thinks about how much time until the race. He or she plans out a training program with both short-term and long-term goals. Each day, that person sets out to work on their training in preparation to meet the goal.

The other person, however, sees no value in that type of planning, viewing it as 'overkill.' However, they continue to talk about running the race and even go for a practice run on occasion.

Now comes the few weeks before the marathon. The person who has worked a little bit every day is now running long distances and has conditioned their body through daily training to be fully prepared. The other is in a panic, trying to train all at once for the race. Who do you think will succeed on race day?

Life is very much a marathon, and if you don't prepare yourself daily for opportunities, you won't be ready when they present themselves. Having a clear direction regarding a path toward your best life allows both your conscious mind and subconscious mind to go to work and help make those goals a reality.

No goals, no progress. It is that simple.

Defining Success

Before you start setting goals or getting ahead of yourself, you must define your idea of what constitutes success. I don't mean what others may see as success, such as millions in the bank or the latest sports car in the drive. Now, if those things are what you desire, there's nothing wrong with that. But I will tell you that when most people think about success, it is not a huge pile of money that comes to mind.

For many people, real success is about doing what you want, when you want and how you want. It is freedom. Yes, money is often the path to that kind of life, but when you are defining success for you, think about the life you want to live and what you'd do with your time.

I have studied and worked with a variety of personal development leaders. Almost all of them impress upon their students and clients how important it is to think about the life you want. Imagine what you'd do with your time if money were no object. There are a couple of reasons for this.

We all have certain ideas about money. It defines the kind of life we lead and what we are able to do. It is often the boundary within which we live — so much so that it can be difficult to imagine a life in which money is not a constant concern. This means we edit our hopes and dreams based

Chapter 5

upon what is 'probable' given the financial limitations we have right this minute.

The real dreams of what can be are pushed aside as unrealistic before they even have a chance to be planted in our mental garden. If there is never a seed of hope that a dream is possible, it never will be. The first thing you must do is set aside the financial concerns you have today and dream about what you want and the kind of life you would like to lead.

Now write that dream down in Section 2 in your workbook! This is an important step because one of the biggest factors in achieving goals is personal accountability. Writing things down makes you much more accountable and also solidifies the desire in your subconscious mind. You read what you wrote, think about it, actively write tasks to work on and then review it frequently, even daily.

Remember when we talked about the fact that the subconscious mind takes the information presented by all the senses and stores that information? With this exercise, you are using your imagination as well as physically writing the goal. You are then repeatedly seeing it, and that impression is stored again and again in your subconscious.

It is much like in class when you watched an instructor demonstrate a styling technique. You listened, probably wrote down notes and then tried it for yourself. The first attempt at performing the technique was probably less than perfect. So you watched again, reviewed your notes and practiced. Over time, you conquered that technique and can now perform it with ease.

Design Your Own Path

Your business and professional goals are met in the same way. Let's say you decide you want to improve communication with a fellow stylist in the salon. You write the goal down, learn how to improve communication and take notes on the action steps you will take. As you put those ideas into practice, you may not get everything right on the first few tries. But as you continue to focus on the change you want in that relationship, things improve.

As you conquer a goal, it is added to those you have already accomplished and are now just part of your normal way of being. You don't have to actively stop and remind yourself how to communicate better, you just naturally do it.

Your goals are completely your own, but sometimes the idea of change can be overwhelming. You may be thinking, "I'm not sure what I even want!" This is not a strange or unusual thought. As I said, many people are so used to living life on autopilot they don't entertain what their idea of success might be, or what goals they should set.

In my experience, to define what success is for you, there needs to be a "why." Why are you working right now? Who are the people that are affected by your decisions? What is important to you? As you move through the various stages of your life, the answer to these questions will change, and your goals will too. This is normal and something you can plan for.

For example, if you have small children, many of your goals will include a better life for them as well as yourself. There will be a number of goals focused on work/life balance as they grow. When those children age and leave home, you have much more freedom to set entirely new goals and a

Chapter 5

new definition of success. You may even decide to choose a different career that expands on the knowledge you have gained and more clearly defines where you want to go at that stage of life.

This was my path. I saw the move to counselling as a natural growth from my decades spent communicating with my hairdressing clients. When I first started learning those counselling skills, I tried them with hairdressing clients first. As I became more confident, I used my new skills to help other hairdressers and then salon owners. Now, I coach business people and hairdressers from around the world, both in their professional and personal lives. I coach and lead others to pursue their goals and live their best life, and that only happened because I developed the necessary people skills and grew into that role. I dared to dream a bigger, more fulfilling dream for myself and used my love of the beauty industry as a launching point.

I very much loved being a hairdresser, which is why I am still so involved in the industry. But I realised I could have a greater impact on people's lives by moving from doing hair to counselling and encouraging people to improve their lives. I see impacting the lives of others in a meaningful and lasting way as the ultimate success for my own life.

Your path is yours to create. Start by imagining a better life and what success means to you right now, and write it down. Be as specific as possible, and resist the urge to self-edit. Just write everything that comes to mind and then go back and focus those ideas into a definition of success for you. As you grow to new heights, that dream will grow with you, but nothing you learn will be lost. It will add to everything you do and enhance everything you are or will become.

Getting to the Goals

For many people, setting goals is right up there with budgeting as far as difficulty because it takes so much effort and thought. When I talk about goals, there are two areas of focus, which I've mentioned previously: long-term goals and short-term goals. Long-term means two to five years out, but without a specific end date.

To start thinking long-term, ask yourself questions such as, "Where do you want to be in two years? Five years? How do you want your business to grow by then? What will your personal life look like in five years?

The second area — short-term goals — involves ambitions you have for the next twelve to twenty-four months. These are specific and achievable within that time frame. Once you list those goals, you break down the monthly, weekly and daily tasks to make them a reality, just like that marathon runner.

The whole intent of this process is to develop a long-range vision, which may not have a very sharp focus. However, then you set the very short-term task lists to move you along toward that vision. Each of these short-term lists is much more sharply focused on exact dates for accomplishments and specific actions that must be taken daily and weekly. Without those specific steps, you will find that next year at this time you are in the same place as you are right now.

This also brings up the idea that you don't have to start with giant earth-shattering goals! Let's say that you want to live a more joyful, peaceful life. That is a great long-term goal. So, when you think about the small daily things you

Chapter 5

can change to work toward that big goal, think small and immediate — ideas such as not listening to the negative news each morning. This changes how you feel about each day. Maybe you can rework how your family starts the morning to get everyone out the door with minimal stress.

Perhaps you set a weekly 'check-in' time with your spouse to ensure you are on the same page and communicating well. You might also have small goals to simply ask clients for new referrals or alter your hours on certain days to increase business. It's amazing how willing people are to help if you only ask.

Tiny goals may seem insignificant, but they add up to significant change over time. As you track your outcomes, you can look back and see the difference. Down the road, as you continue to add small tasks and small daily goals to what you are doing, you will see that you have built the joyful, peaceful life you initially dreamed about. It didn't happen all at once, or only because you imagined it. It happened because you worked toward it every day.

When you pick a goal that is overwhelming and then don't make small baby steps to achieve it, you tend to put it off and not do anything. This is when those little goals will save you. It gets you in the habit of achieving something and allows you to feel successful every day. That encourages you to keep going.

The same principles can be applied to your career goals. Imagine those big long-term career goals, and write them down. Let's say one of those goals is to own a salon. Now, think about those small goals that will get you there. How can you learn new techniques? How can you learn the business side of running a salon? How can you get your personal life and finances ready to be an owner versus a working stylist? What goals are you going to set today to get there?

I will insert a quick word of encouragement here. I mentioned in previous chapters that the fear of making a wrong choice can allow that fear to take over. Fear causes anxiety, which so many people carry around like a weight every day. Part of this fear originates with the idea that we must be perfect and make perfect decisions.

Goals are not edicts that are set in stone. They are meant to be part of a living document that grows and changes as you grow and change. A goal you had five years ago may not even be on your goal list today. Not because you achieved it, but because the opportunities you experienced as you grew took you in a different direction. Embrace those changes and follow your heart.

Don't allow perfectionism or rigidity to rob you of the joy of seeing where life takes you. While each one of us wants and needs to strive to improve, a perfectionist attitude will rob you of the joy of those stepping stone accomplishments. When you have a perfectionist mindset, nothing will ever feel good enough, when the truth is that you are going further than you have ever been before.

It is human nature to have a tendency to discredit the wins and focus on our setbacks. Negative information screams into our subconscious, while the positive is just a breeze we often ignore. Don't just focus on the end result like it is some kind of pass/fail test. Experience the journey, as that is the real part of life.

Chapter 5

Success and accomplishments aren't one point in time. They are the culmination of a lifelong effort as you grow and change. You will not only 'get there,' you will immediately surpass that goal and move on to the next one.

One of the most powerful aspects of your journey is writing down your goals and efforts along the way. This gives you a powerful journal of transformation that spans weeks, months, years, even decades. I know several individuals who have kept journals, mastermind notebooks or goal lists from early adulthood forward. While it is easy to look back and laugh at so many goals that were small and easily accomplished, at the time, they loomed large in your life.

When a goal is reached, no matter how large or small, the mind immediately files it away as you move on. Over time, those goals recede into the past and become less significant in our minds. That doesn't take away from the fact that you struggled to get past them.

Having things written down allows you to go back and experience where you were at the time when that goal seemed so large. It brings the feelings of uncertainty back into focus, and you once again feel the joy of having achieved it. If you simply rely on memory, then that goal, and the joy associated with it, becomes quite small.

Even if you only keep a bullet point journal, that is enough to help you focus on your goals and make progress. This books' companion workbook is formatted to help you get started with your goals and track your progress. But I encourage you to make keeping track of your transformation a lifelong habit.

Question Everything

The most difficult task as you set out to design your life is forcing yourself to question every idea or attitude that you now have. You must identify them if you are to make changes. This often means uncovering some difficult or hurtful truths about yourself or about others.

This is not meant to drag you into emotional despair. It is meant to allow you to objectively understand which ideas no longer serve you and then set about replacing them.

Ideas come from everywhere, so it's not about laying blame or delving far into the past. The only person who can change your thoughts and ideas is you. No matter where an idea or attitude originated, this is not about 'fixing' what happened or confronting those in your life. It is about accepting the fact that all you can control is you. Once you realise that, you can then focus on the steps you can take now and in the future to replace negative ideas or thoughts.

As you can imagine, trying to be objective and identifying things you want to change can be a challenge. For this reason, I'm giving you a few areas to investigate to get things going.

The first of these is negative self-talk. What kind of negativity rolls through your mind every day? It occurs so naturally that we often don't even realise it's happening. Stop and think about the negative thoughts you have had in the past twenty-four hours. Write those down. This is not to make you feel bad; it is just to get them on paper so you can effectively deal with them.

Chapter 5

Imagine you have been mentally kicking yourself since you arrived home because you forgot to stop at the grocery store. Maybe there was something you needed for dinner or something you were supposed to pick up. How many times have you thought about the fact you forgot?

Now, stop and question that for a minute. Does it really matter? Does it matter enough for you to beat yourself up? Probably not. If you have to go back to the store, so what?

We are all tempted to discount the fact that we make ourselves feel much worse about small things than we should. It is important to understand that while your mind is focused on something you forgot to do, or maybe something you regret, you cannot focus on enjoying the present. The negative self-talk stops you dead in your tracks and can even set you back.

Ask yourself: Is this worth setting myself back and possibly not getting the life I want? When you put it in those terms, almost any event or issue shrinks and becomes insignificant. That is what you must train yourself to do immediately. Realise forgetting to go to the store is completely insignificant in the grand scheme of where you are going. Simply take care of it and move on.

The same is true with career issues. I have experienced getting upset and angry at a client who yelled at me for doing as they asked. I could have insisted that it wasn't my fault (it wasn't), but does that change anything? Not really.

You must deal with those issues in the moment and move on. The anger doesn't serve you and certainly doesn't change things. You can't allow your mind to dwell on it and continually run "I should have said" scenarios through your mind. Those scenarios only make you feel worse and will never bring any peace or resolution.

This takes practice, especially if you have a habit of being hard on yourself. Accepting and embracing ourselves as human beings means embracing your imperfections. Allow yourself the opportunity to grow and do better.

In the end, negative self-talk is a habit like any other, and to reduce and eventually eliminate it, you must actively replace the negative self-talk with something positive. When you are in a state of mentally berating yourself for something, stop and write it down. Now, replace that negative thought with a positive thought and write it down, marking out the negative thought. It is a symbol to your mind that you are eliminating that old thought and embracing the new. Go back to what you were doing, but now focus on that positive thought every time you are tempted to fall back into negative self-talk.

This includes refusing to hear it from others as well. As a young stylist, I had not yet learned how to keep the comments and negative conversations of clients from affecting me. I had one particular client who would come in every four weeks for a haircut. Every time he came in, he would complain about his last haircut.

Of course, this affected me! I worried I had done a bad job and couldn't understand why he didn't say something at the time. I tried harder each time but felt as if nothing I did would ever be good enough. It got to the point that whenever I saw his name in the appointment book, I became overwhelmed with anxiety— to the point where I would break out in hives with a rash down my neck!

Chapter 5

One day, as I was listening to his normal whining and complaining about the way I cut his hair, I found my bravado. I told him that he was more than welcome to go to another stylist if he wasn't pleased with my work.

At that point, he looked at me and said, "Why would I do that? I love coming to you."

I realised that the complaining was his version of small talk, and he meant nothing by it. However, I had internalised his negativity to the point of getting a horrible rash just at the thought of having to cut his hair.

This taught me that it is better to be upfront and address the negative talk or issues right away. Making assumptions about what people mean allows negative emotions to build that are both destructive and unnecessary. I became much more careful about allowing someone's negative comment to get to me from that point forward.

It can be very hard to accept that the person that often talks about you the worst and actively berates you daily is staring back at you from the mirror each morning. We are undoubtedly our own worst enemies, and when we mentally berate ourselves, we allow others to get away with doing so as well.

Don't allow anyone else to steal your joy. Take it back and replace any negative comment someone makes with a positive one.

These action steps will make an immediate difference in your perception of yourself. Over time, they will also make a noticeable change in the people with whom you interact.

The Value of Integrity

When we think of the word integrity, we think of someone who is authentic and trustworthy. That is because they live life by their own set of principles, no matter the situation or who they are dealing with. Integrity is something that can add a great deal of peace and value to your life. It allows you to gain strength as you become the person you now choose to be.

When we think of integrity, we imagine someone who is honest and has a backbone when confronting difficult situations. Integrity is both of those things, of course, but it is also about honouring yourself and others. It is about respect for who you are becoming and choosing to see the good in those around you.

I do want to caution you here. Living a life of integrity is not about making yourself better than anyone else or judging others. In fact, it is just the opposite. It is about serving others and choosing to see the good when things are terrible. Your focus is to stay out of the drama, gossip and negative mindset that doesn't add to your life.

For all of us who have spent many years in and around salons, it is not necessarily always the best environment for personal growth. Salons can be rife with gossip, office politics and habitual negativity. While it takes a great deal of effort to block such things from your mind, it comes easier with time. That is because you begin to see the benefits personally.

You don't take home those negative feelings or anger toward people. We all know that a bad day at the salon often produces a bad evening at home as you continue to dwell on what happened. Living a life of integrity means taking charge of those emotions and giving the best of yourself to your clients, but also to those you love the most — including yourself.

Doing what is right in any given situation is never easy, but it gives you peace of mind when you refuse to carry around negative baggage. The desire to be a positive, encouraging person to others is a worthy goal, and here again, it makes a difference to the lives of those with whom you work and live.

Personal integrity goes along with professional integrity, which is more than being honest in your dealings with clients and co-workers — although it certainly includes that. This is about respecting those same clients and co-workers.

Respect includes showing up on time, or even early, for appointments or meetings. It includes cleaning your workstation and being considerate and kind to those you encounter. While this may seem to go without saying, it amazes me how many stylists don't understand that this spirit of respect for others is necessary to have a growing, vibrant business.

Take, for example, a busy day at your salon. Clients are arriving, every station is full and things are quite busy. Now imagine you are a client who has come in. What happens if you stand there waiting, and not one person makes eye contact? You wait a while more, and no one greets you or even acknowledges your presence. How do you feel?

Respect means ensuring people feel acknowledged, even on a busy day, greeting them, explaining the timeline and even offering them a place to sit or something to drink means a great deal. It can mean the difference between them gladly waiting for their stylist or angrily walking out the door. I frequently talk about a study that I read years ago that named rudeness as the number one reason clients leave a salon and don't return. Every study made since then lists this same issue (lack of customer service) as the main reason clients don't return.

Rudeness comes in many forms, and this includes how you interact or don't interact with each client. It includes showing them respect in ways such as being on time and contacting them if there is a schedule change. So many of the issues hairdressers experience with clients come down to basic common courtesy.

The same is true of co-workers. Imagine a stylist in your salon who is perpetually late in the morning. You constantly apologise on their behalf, and while that person may say they are sorry, they continue to be late. It doesn't take long for all the stylists in the salon to get fed up with this behaviour — not because it is a big inconvenience, but because it is disrespectful to both the stylists and the clients. This issue is that the stylist comes across as thinking his or her needs are more important than anyone else's when that isn't the case.

To have integrity, you must do what is right, not what is easy. This means ensuring you respect co-workers and clients, even the ones you don't like as a person. If those around you do not do the same for you, remember that integrity isn't about them; it's about you and how you feel about yourself as a person. If you are one who serves people and looks for the good in any situation, you will always have work and

Chapter 5

always be in demand by clients. So, not only does it move you forward personally, integrity adds to your bottom line.

This is also true if you have a salon of your own. Stylists want to know you will treat them all fairly and take care of issues quickly. They want a leader who is wise and doesn't react out of emotion or vindictiveness. They want someone unafraid to jump in the trenches and lend a hand, to lead by example.

Many people assume strength comes from being 'in control.' What they don't realise is that no one can control another person unless that person allows it. By serving those people you work with and showing you care about them as people, they will willingly choose to work for you and with you.

Integrity, honesty and loyalty are closely intertwined. When people use their natural intuition, they can tell if someone is being honest and dealing with them respectfully. They immediately trust those people and, over time, will become very loyal to that relationship. Every stylist dreams of having a lifelong, loyal following of clients. Exhibiting this type of personal integrity is how that starts. You want to be the kind of person, and the kind of professional, that they can put their trust in for the long-term.

Co-workers crave that kind of integrity as well. How many times have you heard of a stylist leaving a salon or going out on their own, and several of their former co-workers go with them? They don't leave out of happenstance; they leave because the loyalty and desire to be around that person is stronger than the culture of the existing salon.

Everyone wants to spend time around people they enjoy. But in a working environment, it is more than liking someone. They must respect each other as individuals and as professionals to have a productive workplace. At the end of the day, stylists will go with the location and the people that create a positive and productive environment.

If you work to create integrity within yourself, it will naturally spill over to the work environment and allow you to create a great team of people that clients can't wait to do business with.

Chapter 6

Make
It
Happen

Chapter 6
Make It Happen

Success is happiness, right? Well, yes and no. We talked in the last couple of chapters about defining what success means to you and then setting goals to achieve those dreams. However, as you travel your own road to success, you must be mindful that you are also creating a happy life.

I know you have heard many times of those individuals or celebrities who seem to have it all, but who are also extremely unhappy. We even occasionally hear of the suicide of one of these people and wonder how could they choose to die when they have everything?

What this points to is the fact that money and material success aren't everything. The whole idea of a happy life is balance. You are working toward your goals, yes. But you must also enjoy the journey and be fully present today. Often, we get so wrapped up in planning for the future or worrying over the past that today passes without notice.

Many people seem to envision happiness as a destination — a place we arrive at when goal A, B or C happens. But

Chapter 6

happiness is not a place or a point in time. Happiness is the feeling of joy we get from our everyday lives. The satisfaction of knowing we are living a life we chose and are accomplishing what we want.

By that definition, it is easy to see why so many people are unhappy. They do not feel they are living a life of their choosing. They may even dislike what they do for a living, but they must do it to pay the bills. We have all been there — in that feeling of being trapped somehow in a life we didn't expect or actively choose.

What you must realise is that you did choose the life you currently live. Your reaction and response to various events or circumstances in your life have brought you to this point. It may not feel as if you had choices along the way, but you did. Once you accept the personal responsibility for where you are, you can then change it. However, when you feel helpless, like a victim with no control over your life, you tend to accept where you are while convincing yourself you are powerless to change anything. This is absolutely not true.

You have the power to change anything and everything about your life, and you must grasp that power to make it happen. This doesn't mean you will have all the answers. You won't. But you can find them either with your own research and personal growth, through mentors, or both.

The first task is figuring out what gives you joy. Maybe you love being a hairdresser, but don't love where you live. Great news, you are not a tree! You can move anywhere and be a hairdresser. If you'd rather live in an urban environment, you can certainly do that. If you'd rather live in the mountains, you can do that as well. One of the best things about being in our profession is that you can do it anywhere. Want to move to the UK or the United States? People need hairdressers there too!

Few professions are so portable. You define where you want to be and what you want your future to entail. But happiness is more than that. Happiness revolves around the people and experiences in your life.

Relationships are Key

We arrive in this world with a defined set of relationships. Family. Family can be both a positive and negative influence in your life depending on circumstances, and they are the one set of relationships that we don't choose. However, we can each decide as we mature if these relationships will be more or less important in our daily lives.

As we move through adulthood, we also create professional and personal relationships outside of our initial family. As we grow, we also create new families and our own circle of influence. As you make decisions about the rest of your life and how you want it to be, you must also look at those relationships and make some decisions.

Some of your relationships are positive, and some may be negative. Now is the time to work on those relationships and improve them as much as you can. Then you can decide who will be in your life going forward, and who will not. Your workbook contains an illustration in Section 2 of a circle of control to help you evaluate those relationships.

I'm not saying you slice and dice your relationships like a cheesecake — far from it. But you must determine which people help move you forward, and which ones don't.

Chapter 6

For example, let's say you regularly go out on Friday nights with a group of co-workers. You have a few drinks, talk and laugh, but a great deal of the talk is negative. You talk about or make fun of clients, other hairdressers or people you know. You realise that this social interaction is not only negative, but it is also keeping you from other more positive social interactions every Friday night. While you may still feel as if you occasionally need to go out with coworkers to maintain some goodwill, you can choose to limit those nights out to perhaps once per month so that you can spend time with more positive and supportive people in your life.

The opposite is also true. You may feel completely isolated and have very few friends and almost no support system. What then? I will say that there are times when we all feel somewhat isolated. Often this is due to specific circumstances within our lives.

I remember my time as a single mum and how isolated I felt. I had very little time to spend with friends and no money to do so if I wanted to. I felt I had no choice but to work long hours and then sit at home alone. But that was not reality. Many other single-mum hairdresser felt the same way. I could have easily connected with a couple of them and shared free babysitting or enjoyed a few nights together each month. However, I didn't feel like I had any power to change things back then. I had convinced myself that this was my lot in life, and I had to endure it until things somehow improved.

You can choose to find solutions for every issue in your life, but you must pay attention to those areas for certain solutions to manifest. When I say manifest, I mean that they will show themselves. Remember, in an earlier chapter, I talked about how those solutions are always there, but you can't see them because you aren't looking. You have your head down, convinced that life is the way it is. Only when you seek to discover a better, happier life, will those new ideas come forth and allow you to change.

The Wheel of Life

To understand how to balance your life better, I have included a wheel that shows some of the major areas of life that need your attention. Now, obviously, not everything will have equal weight during various times in your life. There are times when your children take more time. There are times when your career must have precedence and even times when leisure time is more important. The goal is to figure out the right mix for you at each stage of your life and adjust as necessary.

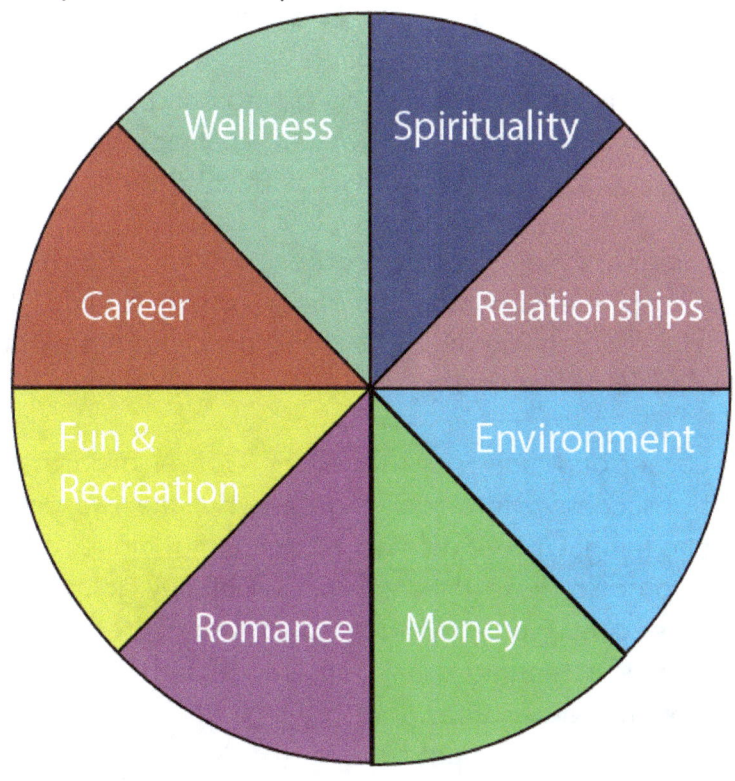

Chapter 6

What you can't do is delete entire areas. Part of being human is the need for fulfillment in all these life sectors. If one area gets shut down or ignored for too long, it can have devastating effects. Things such as career burnout are caused by other areas in your life not getting the time and attention necessary for you to be happy and fulfilled.

I know that early on in my career, especially as a young salon owner, there were many things I neglected. I didn't have the skill set to juggle all the responsibilities, nor did I understand the importance of balance. There were times I worked seemingly around the clock and was so exhausted I wasn't even sure if I was in my life, let alone anyone else's!

It is critical to sit down a minimum of once each year and evaluate how you are doing in each area. I recommend at least quarterly, but yearly is a minimum. The point is to compare where you were at this time last year for that area, what progress or wins you have had and where you want to go. This process allows you to track the positive forward motion and stay on track with your goals.

These eight areas include career, wellness, spirituality, relationships, environment, money, romance and fun/recreation. When you think about these various areas, there are a few important things to note.

First, career and money are separate. Career progress and financial success often track together, but the two are not the same thing. Career affects the amount of money coming in, but you also make the decisions on money going out. In the career area, you may have goals such as becoming an instructor or attending a big conference; but in the money area, you may have other goals such as purchasing a home or investing for retirement.

Similarly, romance and relationships are quite different. Relationships include coworkers, family and friends, while romance is specific to your love life. We need both types of relationships, and they must be worked on independently. As you gain communication skills in the workplace, you will also want to utilise and hone your skills in communicating with your significant other. In your workbook there is a chart showing the various stages of relationships that will give you clarity on how they evolve.

Wellness is an extremely important area and becomes even more critical as you age. If you physically feel terrible at work or home, it is very difficult to reach your goals or stay positive in any way. This area includes every aspect of good health, from eating healthy foods to getting enough sleep and exercise. How you take care of your body has a direct effect on your mind and spirit.

When I was young, I took a job on Tuesday afternoons at a particular salon. This salon had a lot of powerful, dominating personalities, and at that time, I was a timid, non-confrontational person. The tension between personalities was so intense that it led to what I would today describe as a bullying environment. People were teased or demeaned daily, and I found it very uncomfortable.

Each Tuesday, I would sit outside in my car and give myself a pep talk before entering. I had a knot in my stomach the whole time, and it became rapidly clear that this was affecting my overall health. I had stomach issues and could count on being sick every Tuesday after working in this toxic environment. At the time, I was too timid to up and say this is enough and quit on the spot. So instead, I tried to endure the abuse for another six months. Eventually, I did approach

Chapter 6

the owner and quit, but I struggled with the decision. I felt like I was a wimp for not being able to endure it.

I now know that those feelings I had of being weak for not staying were not true. I simply didn't have the emotional skill set at that moment to deal with that level of toxicity. This was a lesson I learned early on about protecting myself physically. There is no reason to stay in any environment that makes you physically ill, and I haven't done it since. You must commit to protecting your wellness as no one can, or will, do it for you, and it can tremendously affect your spirit.

While we are talking about spirit, let's address the idea of spirituality. For some, this means religion. For others, it is their connection to the universe or nature. I define spirituality as whatever feeds your soul. That could be a thought-provoking book, going to church or even camping under the stars. It is that thing that allows you to breathe deeply and be grateful for another day. We each need to touch base with this part of ourselves and fill our spiritual wells from time to time. When our spirits weaken, we allow exhaustion and illness to creep in and take over.

One of the things that directly affect our spirit is the environment in which we exist. Some of us have experienced extremely toxic work or personal environments, such as I mentioned previously. If you are currently in one, that needs to change as quickly as possible. Manage changes through improved communication and clarity on roles and responsibilities.

However, it is also important to acknowledge that there are times when a situation or a person is so incredibly toxic that you have no choice but to remove yourself. This is part of self-care, too. An extended stay in that situation will eventually break your spirit completely, so you must stand up for you and ensure that the environment you are in is positive and gives you what you need to succeed.

The last area on the wheel is fun and recreation. Our hearts yearn to laugh and enjoy our lives. We can do this in both big and minuscule ways every day. Maybe you plan to take that tropical vacation you've always dreamed of, or perhaps it is something as simple as taking the kids out for ice cream. Either way, it gets you out of the regular routine and opens up your world to joy and living in the moment.

When we are young, we all have a bit of an adventurous spirit that often gets tarnished or forgotten with age. Embrace the adventure in your life, and plan to do something new at least once each month. Maybe it is something as simple as seeing a new movie, taking a cooking class or going on an overnight with girlfriends. Perhaps it is stealing away to a log cabin in the woods to enjoy all the peace that nature has to offer, or making the time to meet a friend for coffee. Whatever it is, keeping in touch with that tiny part of yourself that yearns for adventure contributes a great deal to your enjoyment of life.

Each of these areas has a role to play in overall happiness and deserves to be part of the plan for your life. As you move through your goals, you can evaluate and readjust each area to suit your needs. Once again, I strongly encourage you to write everything down. Write down your money goals. Include the little adventures you enjoy, and make notes on the progress in your relationships. Write it all down!

I have notes and journals from years ago, and each time I look at one, I am amazed at how far I've come in so many areas — much farther than I could have even imagined when I first actively began to improve myself years ago. Give yourself the gift of seeing your progress over time, as it encourages you to keep going and set new goals.

In your workbook and gratitude journal are sections for creating the perfect year that will walk you through the steps I've just described. This is a tool you can use each year to advance along on your path to happiness. The idea is to take the good part of what is working today and build on that foundation for tomorrow. We can all add more happiness to our lives, so no matter where you are on the path, this will only increase your overall satisfaction.

Find a Partner

Nothing helps you accomplish goals more than sharing them with someone who will encourage you regularly. This person can also serve as an accountability partner. Find someone who also wants to grow and change their lives. This could be a mentor who can help steer you toward your goals while they are following their own.

Some search for a group of likeminded people each working toward their individual goals. Called a mastermind group, participants offer each other encouragement when it's needed most and provide ideas that perhaps haven't been thought of before. Having the support of positive people who are making positive changes can be invaluable and allow you to transform yourself faster than if you tried to go it alone. I experience this myself, as I host a weekly mastermind group that helps me and the other members stay on track.

Make It Happen

I feel very fortunate that when I was a young salon owner, I joined a group of other salon owners I knew, and we often got together at events or conferences and had long discussions about products, staffing issues, management ideas and so forth. Being inexperienced and young, I found the advice and support from this group to be valuable.

The salon owners' group gave me confidence that others were going through the same issues I was. It wasn't because I was young or new to owning a salon; they had the same problems and often many solutions that I didn't know of or hadn't experienced. It wasn't that the group had all the answers; they didn't. But they were supportive at a time when I desperately needed that peer encouragement, and we often found answers together. I know things would have been tremendously more difficult without that group, and I am continually grateful for its support. Many of the members became lifelong friends, and we still get together on occasion.

A like-minded group can give you a place to try out ideas, get advice, and develop camaraderie among people who share similar struggles and desires.

Your homework is to think about each area on this wheel and make some plans for improvement. You may already be hard at work on some areas, while neglecting others. Now is the time to aim toward that balance your life needs.

Chapter 7

Work Smarter Not Harder

Chapter 7
Work Smarter, Not Harder

I will say that no matter how hard you work, you will not get anywhere until you learn to work smart. This means you must take the time to plan where you are going, and then take steps to get there. No one can do it for you, but the more you understand about the process, the easier it gets.

"Hustle" isn't Enough

I'm sure you have heard the saying that the definition of insanity is to keep doing the same thing while expecting different results. Many gurus and advisors constantly promote 'hustle.' I have no issue with people working hard, but if you are working hard at the wrong things, then how does that help you?

Not only is it ineffective to blindly work harder without a plan, but it is also unrealistic. We all get tired. As a young person, my focus was on building something that didn't require that I slave away to make a buck every day. I am all about hard work, but I wanted something that paid more than just a wage. I wanted to build a business and then an income stream that would support my goals down the road.

Chapter 7

I had an innate drive to learn more and add to my skills, so I took every class that came along. Later, as a salon owner, I did the same thing. I wanted to know if a better way to do something existed, such as a more efficient way to manage my business. I learned constantly, and I believe it was because I was passionate about the profession. I certainly didn't have the same drive coming up in school! But when it involved being a hairdresser, I wanted to be the best. I wanted my salon to excel, and I knew it would take more than hard work to make it happen.

Hairdressers have a distinct advantage because they can earn money anywhere; people always need the services we offer. However, it is effortless to become complacent and accept the 'good enough' life of today rather than building toward something better for tomorrow.

I can't even tell you the number of hairdressers I talk to that, when asked how they feel about their income, say, "I'm doing okay." What they usually mean is that they are paying their bills (hopefully). What they may not realise is that if they don't invest the time to plan ahead and set some real goals that "okay" life will run out of steam.

One hairdresser named Monica is in her early fifties. She is about to retire to a beautiful home on the beach and live her dream life of surfing and having fun. I asked her how she made that happen.

"When I was in my late twenties and my kids were little, I started having problems with my shoulders. Standing behind a chair all day working on clients was very hard on my rotator cuffs. A doctor told me that, eventually, I'd have to choose a different profession, as I would be disabled by the time I was fifty.

Work Smarter Not Harder

I thought, "What??!", It was a bit of a shock. I guess when you are young, you just think you will be able to work forever, but that was a reality check. I'd poured all my time and energy into becoming a hairdresser and had built a consistent clientele. I didn't want to lose that, but I realised that if I didn't plan ahead, I would get to my forties or fifties with bad shoulders and no way to work.

I decided to focus on expanding my skills into upstyles and specialising in wedding parties to enhance what I was already doing. My husband and I sat down and made a plan, too. We decided that all the money I earned would go to building our dream home on a piece of land his family -owned. He did a lot of the work himself, and it seemed to take forever!

I can't tell you how glad I am we made that plan. If we hadn't, I fear I would have continued as I was. I mean, we got by just fine but didn't think much about the future or retirement. Now, I can look back and see how much further along we are just because we decided to plan things out.

Our home was finished and fully paid for about seven years ago, and we have rented it out in the summers to tourists, creating even more retirement savings. Thankfully, medicine has also progressed, and I had surgery successfully on both shoulders last year. We each plan to retire in the next few months and have the next twenty years plus to do what we love, which is play at the beach! I could never have imagined that we'd live that kind of life or that I'd ever have been able to retire early and live in a paid-for luxury home."

Monica's story illustrate that each person has their own idea of success or some dream they want to fulfill. But, you

Chapter 7

have to make a plan for it to happen. It's not about just getting a temporary 'side hustle' to pay today's bills. It's deciding what you want your life to look like in twenty years and then creating a plan to get there.

My dream early on was to own a salon. Once I'd done that, my dream changed. I wanted to teach and be on stage with some of the beauty industry's best. I worked and added to my skill set, including becoming well known for upstyles. When I was in my mid-twenties, it was decided that the town I lived in was large enough for a TAFE school of hairdressing. They brought in teachers from the outside, and I got to know one of them quite well. One day she called and told me she was going through a terrible divorce, and she couldn't teach her class that week. She asked if I could teach in her place. I agreed, and when I asked what I should teach, she said, "Anything."

Having owned my salon for a number of years, I'd had plenty of experience training new hairdressers, so I led her class through some basic skills. It went well. She called the next week, and I did the same thing. This fill-in type work continued for quite a while. Eventually, they approached me to teach a night class on upstyles.

That led to a part-time position at the school and to fifteen years of teaching young hairdressers. I would have never been able to reach that dream and accomplish that goal if I hadn't first dreamed of owning a salon and making it happen.

Once I spent those years teaching, the dream changed again, as mentoring and counselling became my passion. While I can now look back and see how all those things connect, I didn't imagine they were all possible at the beginning. Don't be afraid to outgrow your dreams. We all do. The fantastic part is you then have new, bigger dreams. I did, and you will too.

Emotional Intelligence Mindset

Part of working smarter, not harder, is understanding other people as well as yourself. We have already touched on Emotional Intelligence and how you deal with others. Investing in your ability to understand people, and then knowing how to respond to various situations, will allow you to move forward much faster than if you don't. But there is also an emotional intelligence aspect to your mindset. I like to call this the "Good Enough" mindset versus the "Growth" mindset.

When I say "Good Enough," what I mean is that you convince yourself you are satisfied at least enough to become complacent. This is the perpetual rut that you may find yourself in on occasion. One reason it's called a rut is that once you find yourself there, it is much harder to get out of than you may imagine.

Some gurus and leaders talk extensively about this type of mental inertia. It's as if you've reached a plateau, and you perceive that it is just so much easier to stay there than to dream new dreams or work toward a new goal. Ask yourself how long have you carried around that five or ten kg? You've talked about a diet, but have you done it? How long have you talked about getting more training or trying out a new marketing strategy for the business? Have you written anything down or taken any steps to make it happen? How long have you wanted to make more money? But have you truly thought about how you will do it?

Chapter 7

Somehow when we talk about it, it feels as if we are doing something — but we are just talking, which gets us nowhere. This is why I so strongly encourage you to go through and fill out the workbook guide to this book. It will force you to examine what you are doing now, where you want to go and then set about a plan to get there. Less talk, more action.

So, let's assume for a second that you are not sure if you are in a rut or not. There are a few questions to ask yourself:

1. Do you feel talent or drive to succeed is inborn?

2. Do you feel as if you must prove something to the world?

3. Do you avoid asking for help or feel it's a sign of weakness?

4. Do you tend to be set in your ways rather than eager to try something new?

5. Do you set big goals, but never make a plan to get there?

6. Do you get discouraged when you fail, or react defensively?

If you answered "yes" to more than two of these questions, you might have a tendency toward being a 'rutter.' If you continue along that path, those ideas can severely limit what you can accomplish. This is because they indicate a mind full of limiting beliefs. In other words, you are your own worst enemy.

This means you have limited various areas of your life and have convinced yourself that you must achieve certain things or have certain things to succeed. For example, maybe you are convinced that you have to possess a certain level of intelligence, a certain certification or university degree to succeed. You may also believe that you are stuck with your personality and can't treat people any differently than you do now. Maybe you have convinced yourself that there are only certain roles in life for which you are suited, like working as a hairdresser rather than owning a salon.

The biggest issue is that this sort of mindset can convince you that life is terribly hard and that the world is against you. These mental limitations show themselves as you tirelessly try to prove yourself worthy, yet are frustrated with the lack of progress. A person with a limiting mindset often is obsessed with fairness and blames external sources for their lot in life rather than realising they have the power to change anything and everything about their own existence.

I think all of us have limiting beliefs from time to time, but they don't have to be a permanent part of your life. It is possible to transition from this limited, or 'rut,' mindset to one of growth and happiness. The best part of changing how you think is realising that dream is no longer a dream — it's a goal, and you absolutely can achieve it.

To fix something, you must first acknowledge it and then take action to change. The good news is that change can happen rather swiftly. When you start to develop or expand into a growth mindset, what you focus on is very different. How you feel about your life is altered positively. Part of this comes from removing those obstacles that you had placed in your own way.

This takes some practice, but as you implement a more growth-oriented mindset, it will become part of your natural way of viewing life. It becomes a part of you.

Chapter 7

The first stage in this mental transition is to recognise when those limiting beliefs pop up. For example, when you are faced with a setback or roadblock, you must actively control your urge to blame someone else or react defensively. You must take on a 'no excuses' approach to your own thoughts and focus on solutions. In this way, you actively move forward rather than wallowing in depression or allowing yourself to feel like a victim.

I have used this technique my whole life – especially as an instructor. By that time, I'd advanced quite far in life and had more than twenty years of experience in the field of hairdressing. But there were always those students I couldn't seem to reach. I would struggle and stress over them. What was I doing wrong? How could I explain things better? I actively looked for ways to improve. I even asked other instructors to come into my classroom and work with a few of these students that I seemed unable to reach. I wasn't proud; I just wanted those students to learn.

I know that there is always something new to learn, and that brings me to the next point. Those who are constant learners go much farther in every area of life. Take the initiative to learn those things you don't know right now. Rather than thinking, "Well, I don't know how to run a salon." Find the answers and learn. Take classes, or shadow a mentor. The bottom line is, you must put out the effort.

I have learned that every single person can teach you something, whether it is good or bad. The point is to learn the lesson of what you want to do and how you want to be. Set those big goals and work on them every day. Even by just doing small things, but doing them daily, you advance rapidly. Don't be that goal setter who writes down a list of goals once each year but then never looks at it again. Read it often. Think through your plan. Investigate what might work better, what you need to learn and who can help you.

Remember that no skill you learn is ever wasted. You don't know where your dreams and goals will lead you, and by learning all you can, you may end up learning skills that will help push you well beyond today's goals.

Focus on Gratitude

One of the things that I have based personal and professional growth on is gratitude. No matter if you are feeling great about your life right now or are just wondering how you got to be such a hot mess, the ability to focus on the things that are good in your life is very powerful.

The title of this chapter is Work Smarter, Not Harder. You may be wondering how gratitude plays into that. Gratitude is essential for a growth mindset. Now, I'm not going to say that you must always 'be happy.' That false, fake happiness never lasts, and I will be the first to admit there are times life is truly difficult. That is not what I'm talking about when I say to focus on gratitude.

In addition to a workbook, this book also has a companion gratitude journal. This allows you to write down each week what you are grateful for so that you can review it every day. This isn't to somehow brainwash yourself into happiness. This is to show you how, even when life is at its darkest, there are many things for which to be grateful. They may include family, friends, our health, our work or any of the hundreds of things that we take for granted.

Our minds tend to focus on the small irritations or obstacles we encounter during the day. This can put us into a very negative mindset, and as I said before, what you focus on tends to expand.

If you think you are going to have a bad day, you will. If you assume your clients are going to be difficult, they will be. By focusing on the negative, it can actually increase those negative issues you want to avoid.

However, by consciously changing that mental script and intentionally focusing on the good in your life each day, your experience changes. You see the good in others. You are happier, and those little irritations become fleeting incidents hardly worth a thought.

Don't ignore those difficulties; instead, change your perspective. When you focus on little things, you become a small, nitpicky, difficult person. On the other hand, when you take a step back and are grateful for the big picture, which is your life, you become a bigger, more caring person. You are able to put those small things in their proper perspective rather than allowing them to consume your mind unnecessarily.

This is the power of gratitude — the power of perspective. We've touched on perspective before, but being grateful and keeping a gratitude journal is a concrete way of changing your perspective quickly and easily for the better.

Chapter 8

Connections

Chapter 8

Connections

Our connection to others in our lives is more valuable and important than any business or life adventure. Some individuals may float through our lives temporarily, while others remain. Either way, the ability to create meaningful connections quickly and sustainably adds to your life and your business.

If you remember, early on in this book, we talked about the different types of people and how they communicate. Here, we can use that knowledge to enhance your life and their experience with you.

One reason I will be spending a whole chapter on this is that to succeed and be happy, you must know how to create real, valuable connections that go beyond just getting along with others or communicating simply to be understood. Early on in my life, I found this to be very difficult. Had I known then how essential it is, I would have spent much more time learning the nuances of connection.

As we discussed earlier, some people are more naturally outgoing than others. But that is not what I'm talking about here. No matter your natural communication style, you

Chapter 8

can learn techniques to expand your ability to connect. This means fitting your style to the other person, not just expecting them to take you as you are.

I have also talked about how important it is to be your authentic self. In this chapter, I will show you how to do both – how to be that authentic version of yourself while also accommodating another person's communication style. While it will take some time to master, you can implement these techniques immediately, and I guarantee that you will reap immediate benefits.

The Best Version of You

Depending on who we are talking to, we can be different people. Your family gets one version of you, and your friends get another. Clients and coworkers receive yet a third. This doesn't mean you are fake or false; it simply indicates a different comfort level and communication style within each group. This is natural for everyone. The more comfortable you feel, the less guarded your conversation.

Now is the time for you to decide on the best version of yourself for each of these groups. We can all take our communication up a step – something as simple as relaying a positive comment prior to delivering negative news can have a huge impact. We tend to be much less guarded and less 'nice' to those we love the most. But you can choose to rethink this habit.

Ask yourself: how did I speak to my children this morning? My spouse? My parents? When you think about it, these people often get the worst version of you. This realisation won't help you feel better about yourself.

The same is true in the workplace. Once you step foot into the salon, how do you communicate? Do you bring all your troubles, worry and stress from home and unload those on clients and coworkers? You have the power to choose the state of mind you will have going into the day. Do you overshare every detail of your childhood and life, then get angry when people talk about you? This is one reason it is so important to start the day with gratitude. It changes your perspective and view of the world and allows you to release those negative emotions, so they don't infect the rest of your day.

I use that wording because negative feelings are very much like a virus. If one person is in a horrible mood, it tends to rub off on those nearby. But what if it isn't you but someone else bringing that negativity to your work or home?

This is very common, and some days are certainly better than others. I have had extremely negative clients, and it doesn't seem to matter what you do or say, they will spin it to the negative.

One of the things I had to learn early on was a practice of emotional protection. As a very young person in business, I tended to take on, or be affected by, every emotion that I encountered. If someone was sad or had an unfortunate event happen, I was sad. If they were angry, I became angry. While this is a normal empathetic human response, it can negatively impact your life as you encounter so many emotions during a single day.

I quickly learned that empathy and emotional energy are very different things. You can empathise with someone, but you must protect your own emotions and emotional energy

Chapter 8

or they will drain you completely. I would often arrive home in those early days completely exhausted. Not physically, but emotionally, from allowing other people's issues to drain my energy.

You must protect that energy and allow the emotion to roll off. Otherwise, you become a permanently exhausted version of you that no one wants to be around – including you! The best advice I can give is not to ever allow anything in the workplace to upset you. Nothing you will experience in that space is lasting or life-altering. It isn't important enough to allow your mental wellness to be affected.

You can start the day imagining that your emotions are safe and happily playing in a walled garden. You decide what is allowed in that garden throughout the day. When you feel your blood pressure rising from anger or something someone said, imagine that garden wall. You actively decide to leave that issue outside the gate and move on to the next client. That's it.

I have heard a number of people say that they can't 'fake' their emotions. I'm not asking you to. I am showing you that you choose your emotions. When someone says they can't help the way they feel, they are really saying that they choose not to control their own emotions. You absolutely do have that power, but if you actively choose not to use it or exercise it, things will never improve. Understand, that is an active choice on your part; you are not helpless when it comes to your own emotions.

I'm not saying you will never be emotional. You will be, but it will be much more in control. Where once I was an exhausted, emotional person daily, it is now quite rare that my emotions get the best of me. When they do, I can usually pinpoint the presence of an extreme amount of stress. I know that I must address the stress to come back to a balanced state. We will talk more about reigning in stress in the next chapter, but for now, understand that you have much more control over your thoughts and emotions than you realise.

Striving for Better

There is a quote by Maya Angelou that says, "Do the best you can, but when you know better, do better."

I get that; I really do. I look back on my younger self and am almost embarrassed at how badly I handled some situations and relationships. But I also realise that I was doing the best I could at the time. I also am grateful for those experiences because they motivated me to learn more about people and communication. Once I had that knowledge, I did better.

That is the point of this book — to encourage you to grow and address those things about yourself that you have the power to improve. As we discussed, you must first decide what you want to change. Let's say you want to start each day with a smile and a good mood. This is a great goal as it sets the stage for the day. You take a deep breath before you enter the salon and focus on things for which you are grateful. Then, you greet everyone with a smile and ask how they are. No matter their response, you don't allow any negative emotion over your garden wall and look forward to your first client as you ready your station.

This is important because when you first start trying to improve your outlook, you notice how negative others can

Chapter 8

be. That is why visualising the garden wall is so important. I used to hang pictures or posters on the walls that gave me a sense of calm and inspiration, and you may find this helpful as well if it is allowed in your workplace. Inspirational quotes, pictures of the ocean or a calm countryside not only help you refocus your emotions, but they also help your clients to do the same.

As you chat up clients, you don't have to worry about carrying the conversation. Generally speaking, people love to talk about themselves or their lives, so asking a question here and there can allow them to feel heard without you feeling as if you must constantly chatter. In fact, too much chatter on your part can damage the relationship.

As you think about improving your communication style, it is important for you to also commit to talking less and listening more. People have a deep desire to be heard, even on relatively unimportant issues. So talk less, and be sure they know they are heard.

A great technique counsellors often use is to repeat something the client said back to them. This lets people know you are listening closely to what they say and trying to understand them. For example, if they say something about having a birthday party for their husband's sixty-fifth birthday, you can simply say, "I had no idea he was sixty-five!" You aren't talking about you or carrying the conversation; you are letting the person know you heard them. That tends to encourage clients to keep chatting while you focus on their hair.

This is also a useful tool with coworkers you spend a great deal of time around. In the workplace, it is usually better to share less personal information about your life rather than

Connections

oversharing. Many times, issues arose at my salon because various staff members got to know each other a little too well and then had a falling out. Less is definitely more. But how do you do that with people with whom you spend eight to ten hours a day?

One technique I use is the same one I have already talked about using with clients. Repeat things back to them to let them know you heard them. Ask questions, but don't overshare what's going on in your own life. They will not realise that you know much more about them than they know about you.

Remember, these individuals are coworkers, not necessarily close friends. You will move on eventually, and you will never see many of these people again. It is important to protect your own emotions, and the fastest way to get hurt is to overshare personal information with someone who you find out later can't be trusted. This damages both the relationship and the work environment.

I think we have all been in salons where the atmosphere could use a step up in professionalism. Part of that professionalism is focusing on the clients rather than gossiping about each other. You can make the decision for you no matter what anyone else does — being more professional will allow you to shine more and keep you out of the drama swirling throughout the salon. Those two things alone make it very worthwhile.

A much harder area is that of family and friends. They may be used to you being emotional or negative. But that doesn't mean you can't change. I will be the first to say that those closest to us know exactly how to push our emotional buttons. While you may need to limit exposure to them while

Chapter 8

you are working on you, eventually they will see the positive change. It is important to make communication a priority, as it makes every single area of life better.

Now is the time to talk a little about baiting. I use this term to mean those times when someone tries to get you dragged into negative gossip or an emotional discussion. They may say things to get you to react, and this is purposeful on their part. If you are trying to improve, often those around you feel worse. They feel as if you trying to better yourself is an indictment of their own behavior. So they try to pull you back down.

I frequently hear the story of the crab bucket from various thought leaders. Crabs, when put in a bucket, rather than help each other climb out, will instead pull those trying to escape back down. So it is with people in your life. They may not even realise they do it, but subconsciously they may feel that you seeing a need for improvement means they are terrible people who need improvement too. However, they don't want to improve, so they try to get you back into your old routine. If you take the 'bait,' they then make fun of your attempt to be better.

Unfortunately, this kind of behavior can come from those you love the most, which is why I say you may need to distance yourself from them, at least temporarily. Once you have more confidence in the changes you are making, you are more able to withstand the emotional attacks. Eventually, you will convince them you have changed, but don't expect them to accept it just because you say so.

Believing is the real key to your commitment to self-improvement, and it is crucial to stay on that path, no matter what. Gaining control of your emotions allows you to take time to respond and think about what you want to say rather than allowing anger to run rampant. By stopping and thinking, you have much less chance of saying something that requires an apology later.

Approximately 80% of all communication is non-verbal, and you must be aware of that fact. If you say one thing, but your body language says something different, people will see you as inauthentic. Eye contact is one of the most important aspects of communication from a body language standpoint.

Let's say you are slightly annoyed at a coworker and they then ask if you are okay. You may say, 'yes' but refuse to meet their eyes and instead go on with what you are doing. Do you think they believe you? No, they don't. There are many clues you give off when you are emotionally stressed, and though you may think you hide it well, you don't. No one does.

It is important to address the underlying issue, such as getting your own emotions under control. You can't be happy when you are an emotional mess. But when you have the ability to allow all that chaos to swirl around you without effecting your emotions negatively, you can then respond to clients and coworkers positively, and they will know you mean it.

Details Matter

Consistency is important, but you also must allow yourself to stumble toward that happiness you want to achieve. No one does it perfectly, and you won't either. Allow yourself the room to fail one day, but get back on the right path the next. We never lose as long as we advance toward what we tell ourselves we want.

Chapter 8

The interesting thing about improving communication is that it's all in the details. Meeting someone's eyes as they speak, smiling at them, repeating back something they said – these are all very small things, but they make a tremendous impact. As I said earlier, every person wants to know that they are heard. For this reason, I have kept mental notes for years on clients, co-workers and even friends.

Knowing the details about someone allows us to communicate better with them. I know their birthdays, their children's names and even their pet's names. While you may think these items are insignificant, they are quite profound. For someone you may only see a few times per year, it is a big deal that you know their dog's name.

Detailed, personal information about a client is just as important for me to know as the exact color formula they prefer or the cut they like. It reinforces our connection even if we spend very little time together over the course of a year.

The small details in our body language, and the ability to listen and remember, give people a very different impression of us. We have the ability to make them feel important, and they take away from each encounter the fact that we are great communicators.

This is the power that communication has and can bring to our lives. It allows us to deflect the negative and refocus conversations to the positive. This is not all that easy sometimes. I had one very negative older client when I was in my late twenties. She was extremely challenging, to the point I wished she would get another hairdresser! However, through the course of her regular appointments, I found out she had a tiny terrier named Sammy that she absolutely adored.

Once we had that first chat about Sammy, I was amazed at the difference in her behavior. She went from scowling and complaining to laughing and smiling as she recounted Sammy's latest antics. I made it a point from that day on to ask about Sammy every time she came to me, and she became an absolutely delightful client. I believe that she enjoyed the appointments much more as well.

These are the small clues that you must pay attention to that can improve your overall daily life. The great part is that this is a section of your life over which you have 100% control. You can choose to cultivate those relationships, and then you reap the reward.

This includes the idea of gratitude. Let your clients, coworkers and other people in your life know that you appreciate them. Give them a simple 'Thank You' and see the difference it makes. Thank them for their business, tell them how much you enjoy seeing them on occasion or how much you enjoy hearing about their Sammy!

Everyone wants to be appreciated, and simply saying it is enough. That is much more than most people get these days. As you tell someone you appreciate them, it also allows your mind to focus on how important these relationships are to you. The small disagreements and issues don't matter so much and can be easily set aside if you keep your focus on how grateful you are that this person is in your life.

We must always remember that clients can have their hair done anywhere, by anyone. But they will choose to come back to the stylist that they feel hears and know they are appreciated. Those two simple things will do more to grow and sustain your business than any amount of marketing ever could.

Chapter 9

Pulling Your Hair Out

Chapter 9
Pulling Your Hair Out

Not everything in your life will go well all the time. You may be fired, get divorced, lose a loved one or suffer through difficult economic times. I realise this is not news to you. Yet, how you choose to deal with stress in your life, be it temporary or ongoing, determines how you feel about your life. The real truth is that it doesn't matter what the stressor is, but how you handle the stress that matters most.

I go back to the idea that some people whose lives are a huge mess are still upbeat and joyful, while some who seem to have it all are depressed and unhappy. Much of this directly relates to how each person handles stressors in their lives. The ability to effectively manage stress has a tremendous impact on how successful you will be over the long term and how you will feel about your life.

It's important to note that not all stress is bad. Sometimes stress allows us to perform better in given situations, and this can produce positive results. Viewing stress as helpful allows you to access the biology of courage where fear is set aside. Often, stress allows us to connect with others through a shared experience, and this creates resilience.

Chapter 9

While no one wants more stress in their lives, if we can view certain tense situations as having a positive result, it allows us to become much more courageous, resilient and connected individuals. So while you may be experiencing something you currently perceive as negative, if you can see the greater outcome of the situation as positive, it allows you to actively gain from it.

For example, if you are in a bad relationship and choose to leave to better your life, there's no way of saying that the split won't create a horrible mess for a time. However, if you see the future outcome as something positive, you better endure the stress and turn it to your advantage.

While we all strive to achieve that 'life balance' where we simply love being alive, sometimes life is uncooperative. There are circumstances you can't control, and even if you could, sometimes you must choose to upset people or make unpopular choices to move forward.

I think of the time I had a marriage fall apart. I live in a small town, so his relatives and mine took sides, of course, as they often do. There were rumors all over town, many untrue. It was unbelievably stressful. I recall lying awake at night, the nasty comments running through my head like huge herds of wild beasts. I was angry at what was happening and how things developed, but I had no real outlet or way to control it. As anyone who has gone through a similar situation can attest, that anger built into tremendous stress. I recall waking up exhausted and then later falling into bed exhausted, hoping for a few hours of sleep when I wasn't bombarded with negative thoughts.

I was also a single mum, and so I didn't have the option to be emotionally self-indulgent and withdraw from life until things blew over. I had to deal and get on with life. In that respect, my work saved me. It was something I was good at and could depend upon. It was the positive beacon that allowed me to become resilient in the face of something negative. I could set aside my thoughts and emotions, at least for a time, to do the one thing that still made me feel worthwhile.

However, it was a very trying time that I remember vividly because of the stress load I carried like a huge weight every day. I also remember the experience because it was the first time I actively worked to reduce the stress in my life. This was out of survival, no doubt, but the lessons stuck and stress became something I have been hyper-aware of since.

No matter your current situation, understand that you will go through trials that cause you not only immense emotional pain but tremendous tension as well. Actively learning the tools to use to deal with stress and improve your perception of it will give you much more peace throughout your life. While no one can completely remove daily stress, it can be actively reduced and managed to work in your favor.

Stress Affects Everything

We all know that stress affects us physically and mentally. What we tend to underestimate, however, is its detriment to our wellbeing in the long term. Often, we ignore or downplay our stress, but it shows. No matter how much we try to hide or pretend it's not a big deal, it does manifest in our lives, and allowing it to continue in a negative fashion over the long term is not only detrimental, it can literally shorten your life span.

Chapter 9

Stress is defined as a state of mental or emotional strain or tension resulting from negative or very demanding circumstances. Often the effects of dealing with these issues aren't noticed at first but develop into more serious problems over time. You may blame a cold or allergies for a constant headache or inability to sleep rather than growing stress. Instead of attributing your lack of productivity at work to that same stress, you may claim to be distracted for some other reason. But stress can be the root of all these issues and lead to long term health problems such as high blood pressure, heart disease, stroke, obesity and diabetes — just to name a few.

Some of the physical signs of stress are obvious such as a pounding heart or palpitations, stomach upset, fatigue, headache and sleep problems. However, the emotional problems that result can ruin your outlook on life and the relationships you have with others if you aren't careful.

Stress alters your mood through anxiety, a feeling of overwhelm, lack of motivation, sadness or even anger. These behavioral manifestations are what others around you will notice. It could include things like angry outbursts, social withdrawal, indulgence in things like overeating, drug and alcohol misuse or increased tobacco use. These are signs that something is going wrong in your life, and you are trying desperately to cope.

Unfortunately, many people use extremely unhealthy coping mechanisms, and this compounds their problems rather than solving them. These people don't see a way to turn that stress toward the positive, and the spiral continues downward.

One hairdresser I worked with was extremely stressed on a constant basis. She and her spouse fought about money, and there was ongoing tension in the salon due to personality conflicts she had that never seemed to end. Everywhere she turned, life was in turmoil.

This hairdresser was also a very proud person, so she told everyone she was 'fine.' She got through each day and often cried herself to sleep as she felt trapped and overwhelmed by all the negativity in her life.

As I've said before, the first step to solving a problem is to admit it exists. She had to open up to people in her life and talk about all the things that were negatively affecting her. At that point, it was a process to take the problems one by one and work through possible solutions to find healthier coping mechanisms. This type of isolation is somewhat human nature. We hide our pain instinctively. But to cope well, you must connect with others and allow that connection to support you.

One of the biggest stressors each of us face is the knowledge that we need to change something in our lives and yet feeling absolutely powerless to do anything. That frustration isn't something you can set aside or assume will go away. It builds and can add to the sense of being overwhelmed because you feel unable to help yourself. This is where connection offers its worth. It allows you not to feel so alone so that you can get help early and often to lessen the stress you are experiencing.

There is no such thing as a stress-free life, so the goal isn't to eliminate every bit of it. The goal is to learn various tools and techniques that will allow you to use that energy to

Chapter 9

change things rather than allowing it to make you unhealthy, both physically and mentally.

Stress Skills

There are various learned skills that will help you reduce or deal with ongoing stress. Every person has to use what works for them, but most people find these tools effective in various situations.

It is important to remember that stress, just like trauma, is cumulative, so allowing stress to pile on top of stress compounds and amplifies both physical and mental issues. I would encourage everyone to start utilising these techniques immediately, even if you don't currently feel much tension. The reason is to train your subconscious mind to respond when stress does increase in your life, as it will from time to time.

We get used to a certain amount of ongoing tension while still functioning decently. It is only after you implement some of these ideas that you discover how large a stress load you are actively carrying. You will be amazed at how much better you feel once you decrease your current ongoing level. This is especially important to your productivity from a business standpoint.

Many people feel frustrated that they can't get more done each day, and this adds to other stressors, such as a lack of money. By reducing overall worry, many people are surprised at how much better their focus is at work and how much more they can accomplish on any given day. This produces a cascade effect of good through your life. The more you get done, the more money you can make. The more money you can make, the better you feel about where your life is going. The better you feel about where your life is going, the more positively you interact with others in your life, and so on.

Exercise

I'm sure you have heard many times how effective exercise can be to combat stress, anxiety and depression. The problem for some is that they are so stressed they can't figure out where to squeeze one more minute out of the day, let alone make time to exercise.

I want you to consider that exercise doesn't have to be an hour long marathon to be effective. It can be as simple as a quick ten-minute walk around the block or to the coffee shop. It can be a stroll through the park or your neighborhood at the end of the day. It doesn't have to be a sweaty gym experience unless you choose it to be.

The reason exercise is so very effective is that it allows you to disconnect, if only for a short time. You put your mind on autopilot and focus on the walk, the scenery and your body. This disconnect breaks that constant hum of overthinking and worry. Just getting away from everything and everyone provides an immediate sense of calm and peace. This allows you to go back and face the issues at hand with a renewed perspective.

It also helps your body feel better. One of the big factors in the amount of stress you experience is how your body feels physically. Getting the muscles moving and endorphins naturally flowing gives you a little mood lift, which helps everything.

Chapter 9

Eating Well

Feeling better, both physically and emotionally, is directly connected to what you eat. When we are busy and stressed, we tend to grab what's easy, not what's good for us. This may mean fast food or treats brought to the office. Either way, an overload of sugar and carbs makes us physically tired and less alert. So does overloading on caffeine!

Eating well does not mean being a militant foodie. It just means making better choices each day — not necessarily perfect choices — but better choices. Maybe for you, this includes a lighter lunch of protein, nuts and salad while avoiding sugary, caffeinated drinks. This will allow you to sail through the afternoons without becoming exhausted and running the risk of lashing out at others because you don't feel well.

Each person has to learn what works for their body and circumstance, but skipping meals or grabbing something fast can be extremely detrimental in the long-term to your overall health. This is especially true as you age. How you eat and what you eat has a much greater effect on each successive decade of life, especially if you have any underlying health issues.

Food has a direct impact on your emotional and physical wellbeing, so it's important not to discount this area when you are managing the stress in your life.

Sleep and Overall Rest

One of the big indicators of stress is the inability to sleep, or lack of restful sleep. Stress affects thoughts and doesn't allow the mind to 'turn off' at night, so when you are significantly stressed, you can also become exhausted. Fatigue can cause both physical and mental breakdown, as things become much harder when you are tired.

Much like slogging through a pond full of peanut butter, your mind doesn't function as sharply when you are tired, and even mundane tasks seem to take forever. This one factor can substantially lower productivity in every area of your life.

I mention this aspect of stress management third because how much exercise you get, as well as what you eat and drink, affects your sleep patterns. They are all interconnected. When you have issues sleeping due to stress, the first thing to do is get out and get some exercise. Next, look at your diet. Are you consuming a lot of sugar or caffeine? If so, cut those down or out completely, as that will allow your mind to rest more easily at night.

Most importantly, make time to rest and sleep! I will confess, I am the queen of burning the candle at both ends – especially when I owned a salon and was a single mother. I was constantly juggling the various things I had to accomplish, and often the thing that got cut the most was time to rest.

Rest includes not only sleep but also down time during the day when you aren't all go, go, go. When you take a step back, take a deep breath, close your eyes and relax for a few minutes.

It's important to make time to rest, even if you must actively schedule it in. A major step toward that balanced life is making rest and relaxation a priority. It allows you to come back to your tasks refreshed and much more productive. I know for a fact that it is better to be productive and work hard for eight hours, then it is to work ten or twelve hours and feel exhausted.

Step Back/Say No

Most of us pack every minute of every day with things we feel we must do. The second we start running late or feel somehow 'behind' on our task list, our stress immediately escalates. This is largely our own doing in thinking we can, or need to, accomplish far more each day than is possible.

While some may say they do this purposely to accomplish more, what truly happens is that you constantly feel bad that you aren't accomplishing enough. Rather than be happy with everything you accomplished that day, you feel disappointed. But this feeling is one that you have created in your mind. It's not reality.

It is a good exercise to step back and look at all the things you have going on or are trying to accomplish during a particular week. Most people can easily eliminate ten to twenty percent of the tasks they try to do either by delegating them to someone else, consolidating them into groups to be more efficient, or realising they aren't that important.

Step back or say no to things that don't align with your goals and don't agree to tasks to make someone else happy. If you frequently evaluate everything you are doing, you will get in the habit of saying 'no' upfront to those things that you know don't fit into your life. In this way, you can stay on track and ensure you have time for those things that do matter. Stress forces you to prioritise your life, and that can be a very good thing when you eliminate those things that aren't working for you.

Communicate Proactively

This comes back to my favorite topic, communication. By communicating proactively with those in your life, you can easily head off stress and keep things positive. Rather than arguing with your spouse over money or other issues, take a proactive approach and talk together about solutions. Making a plan reduces everyone's stress and manages expectations, so when problems do arise, they can be dealt with openly rather than dissolving into an argument.

Communication also reduces stress in the salon. Having a set meeting each week to discuss issues or ways to do things better allows open communication and proactive conflict management. Unfortunately, many salon owners only have this type of meeting when there has been a big blow up, and it is much more difficult to mend relationships after things are said and feelings hurt.

Focus on being proactive in your communication with others. You will lower the stress points in every area of your life and will reap substantial rewards. This includes paying attention to and eliminating your triggers. One of my clients told me that a huge daily stress trigger for her is just getting the kids out the door on time. While this may seem insignificant to some, starting the day with everyone yelling and screaming at each other set a negative tone for her whole day, as well as that of her children.

Chapter 9

On top of the stress of the moment, she also felt extreme guilt because she thought she was a terrible mother. This happens to a lot of us when we lose our cool with our kids, but it is a situation we can do something about.

I recommended that she make a habit of doing more prep the night before, deciding on clothes, locating shoes and gathering school things in one place. These suggestions made a huge difference, and though they may seem obvious to others, when we are in the depths of our own stress, it can be difficult for us to see solutions. That was the case with this young mother. The stressful mornings had become how they did things, and the solutions weren't necessarily obvious.

Take it Easy on Yourself

My client's situation brings up another issue. Often, we add stress to our lives because we are so hard on ourselves. Those of us with perfectionist tendencies suffer in this respect. We constantly convince ourselves we aren't good enough, didn't do things right, or chose poorly – or perhaps some other emotion that highlights how horrible we are.

Again, this is a creation of our own minds. Only by focusing on the good and talking about our issues can we then find solutions. This includes how we feel about ourselves. Every person has some unresolved emotion, and being able to confront that and deal with it, allows you to progress much faster.

Allow Time to Cope

If you calm the stress in your life today and six months later feel overwhelmed, it's not because you are horrible or less

Pulling Your Hair Out

than anyone else. It simply means that stress is, and will always be, part of your life, as it is part of everyone's life.

We all need time to adjust to various circumstances or situations and find solutions to issues. It doesn't magically happen. We must practice stress management techniques on an ongoing basis to become better at them and to recognise our stress overload.

This is not a 'one and done' kind of situation. Stress will always be in your life, and there will be times you are truly overwhelmed. Those times are when you should seek out a friend or counsellor to allow you to step back and gain perspective. Being close to negative situations removes that perspective, so it's good to have help to see the possible solutions.

Time is interesting in that what seems overwhelming today will be a distant memory or a small blip in the road later on. Our perception is not a true picture of things, but a reflection of emotions we feel right now, and stress heightens those. Over time, they can and will change.

The most important takeaway regarding stress is to understand that you have a great deal of control not only in what stress you allow into your life but also how you manage it. As we talked about in the last chapter, you are in charge of your emotions, and those emotions are affected by stress.

Exercising, eating well and getting rest are only a few of the ways you can combat stress and improve your life dramatically, right now in the short term. As you learn better communication techniques and how to say no to people demanding your time, you will lower the ongoing tensions in your life for the long-term.

While it may feel like the idea of a 'balanced life' is just a myth to you right now, gaining control of stress and anxiety will push you much farther to making it a reality. While stress never completely goes away, you are in charge of ensuring it doesn't rule your life. It is up to you to turn that stress into something positive and use it to create the life you want.

Chapter 10

Living The Dream

Chapter 10
Living The Dream

There is no question that our lives come full circle. Yours will, just as mine has. If someone had told me years ago that I'd be a professional counsellor today, I would never have believed it. I had so many goals and dreams early on – which I accomplished one-by-one over the years. Each built upon the next and led me on a path I would not have ever considered for myself. No one is more surprised than me that I have arrived at this point.

I had mentors and coaches who encouraged me along the way toward each successive goal; to them, I am exceedingly grateful. Especially to that professional counsellor years ago who said the magic words, "You are so much more than just a hairdresser." He was right, and what he said is true of all hairdressers – we are so much more than the job we do. Even after accomplishing my goal of owning a salon, teaching my skills to others, and being recognised as a leader in my field, I know there is more for me to do.

While mine might seem an odd path, the choices I made came down to how I can help people. At first, I learned to help people by making them feel great about themselves through a hairstyle. I loved my clients and became part of

Chapter 10

their lives, as they became part of mine. The same thing happened as I taught new hairdressers the skills I'd learned over the years. I became a part of their lives and their eventual success by helping them learn how to do exactly what I had done.

Being a counsellor requires exactly the same thought process as working with hairdressing clients, although expanded exponentially. I listen and understand, and then offer support and counselling as needed. I now work with business clients, personal clients and, yes, still many hairdressers. Every skill I've ever learned as far as communicating is now invaluable as I lead people toward the dreams that they choose for themselves.

Dream Your Own Dream

Now is the time to ask yourself what dream you choose. As you can see by my story, dreams grow and change over time, so nothing is out of bounds. Once you achieve that first goal or take that first step to improve your life, a bigger, better dream appears that you can also achieve. You may already have some goals and are wondering how to connect the dots to make them happen more quickly and easily. Each one of us runs into roadblocks, potholes and detours, and sometimes those can set us hopelessly off-track. Well, that doesn't have to happen to you.

As I traveled my road, there were many people along the way that shined a light on my path and encouraged me. They were mentors and coaches who shortened my learning curve and kept me from not only making a misstep, but also from getting stuck in the pitfalls that keep so many from living their best life. They held me accountable and refused my excuses that I wasn't good enough, or that something might be too hard for me to achieve.

I learned tough lessons in those early years, and as I've thought about each specific lesson and the people who have taught me, I've developed various programs to address those things I wish I'd known sooner. As you might have guessed by now, many of those programs revolve around improving communication skills, specifically emotional intelligence.

I can look back and see that common thread through most of my past struggles, and I've found that is also true for most people I encounter. Communication hampers so many areas of our lives that until those skills improve, it feels as if you are running in circles.

When I was a new salon owner, for example, oh, the mistakes I made! Most of those mistakes had to do with how I handled people – clients, workers and employees; so one would think it was obvious that this was what I needed to improve. But it wasn't clear to me, and that was because I didn't know better and hadn't been exposed to an easier way. So much of the struggles and stresses I endured during those early years could have been prevented with just a little bit of education on how to deal with people more effectively.

It is interesting that while I was struggling with communication in my work life, I was also having marital problems, as many young people do. It was the same issue in both cases. I had no idea how to resolve conflict or address difficult subjects. Everything ended up in a fight or stony silence. Thankfully, I learned from that situation as well, and now that I've had a successful marriage that has lasted more than twenty years,

Chapter 10

I am extremely grateful for a partner who has been willing to grow and learn with me. However, I know it wouldn't have happened if I had never taken those initial steps to learn about emotional intelligence.

Communication skills can improve every single area in one's life, and it is what I spend a great deal of time addressing with my clients. However, I also know that change is a process, and that we each progress at different rates in different areas.

When I sold my salon and started teaching, I thought I knew a lot about how to communicate. I'd been through so many difficult circumstances and hard lessons that I felt I'd come a long way. But teaching young hairdressers has a way of showing you where you are lacking, and it made me realise how far I had to go. It was a humbling experience for which I am grateful. When you try so hard and yet can't reach that one student after so desperately trying, you know there is much more to learn about people, and it made me want to improve even more.

The secret to getting ahead or leveling up in any area of your life is to understand that you can truly become what you were meant to be. Whether that is in a great career as a hairdresser or some other dream you secretly desire, you can achieve it, but only if you put in the work.

Coaching and Mentoring

I have often had people tell me that they can take a business class and don't see the need for a coach. To me, that's like saying you can teach a football team to play by watching a video. While a class might teach you basic business principles, it won't warn you of all the pitfalls or keep you on track to your goals.

I am a big believer in going to the source, and that means working with someone who has walked the road you are travelling, not just a generic person that has no idea what it's like to be a hairdresser or own a salon! In this way, I function more as a mentor than a counsellor because the businesses and individuals I work with know I have been exactly where they are. I have dealt with the same issues and been successful.

Mostly, they know I won't waste their time. I train their employees to work better together, learn how to be emotionally intelligent and give clients a better experience. With the type of extensive beauty industry experience I have gained over decades, I can achieve excellent outcomes much more quickly than others who may not understand all the nuances involved.

One of my most important functions with business and personal clients is to provide clarity. I frequently meet with people who say they have no idea what their goals should be or what they want. It's common for people to have no idea what their next step in life should be. That one idea causes much more anxiety, in my opinion, than having big goals.

Having no goals at all can be very disheartening. It makes you feel like everyone else has their act together or knows something you don't. Fear creeps in. Other people seem like they are moving ahead, while you are in a holding pattern, going nowhere.

Chapter 10

I work with those individuals to define who they are and what they see as their best life. We discuss their passion and uncover ideas they thought were lost long ago. Sometimes that means just encouraging them that they are on the right path, while other times, it means a complete change of direction for their life.

I recently worked with one young apprentice hairdresser named Judith. She was very discouraged because she had such big plans! There was no lack of dreaming and setting goals for her. She wanted to own a salon and employ a large staff, maybe even have a whole chain of salons one day. I loved her enthusiasm.

The problem was she worked in a salon with a very controlling and overbearing owner — to the point that this owner limited the number of clients she could take and handpicked the clients with whom she was allowed to work. The owner micromanaged Judith to the point she felt her dreams were useless.

I could tell immediately that Judith had the right personality and drive to be a great leader. I worked with her on communication skills. I walked her through how to deal with someone who, though a supervisor, had very little emotional intelligence and therefore did not understand people.

Over time, and through gaining additional skills and understanding, Judith was able to endure the situation and qualify. She quickly moved on to owning a salon and now runs a booming business with seven staff.

I tell her story because it is yet another example of how a situation that seems so dire as to crush a person's dreams can be used to excel farther and faster than if Judith had tried to force the situation without the right skills.

Coaching takes your desires and intentions and helps you lay out a real plan to get there — a plan you can take action on and benefit from as quickly as possible. One of the biggest reasons people fail to accomplish this alone is that they lack motivation and ongoing support.

How many times have you set a goal and told friends and family about it only to get told there's no way to achieve it? A coach is that external, objective third party. They don't bring up your past failures or think of you as an underachieving kid. They support the goals you say you want and help do the hard work — which is the development of the plan.

If you have never achieved a particular goal, how will you know what that plan should contain? You need that objective, professional input to create something that will work and is not just an exercise in futility.

One of the biggest advantages of having a coach is accountability. How many times have you set a goal only to let it go by the wayside when life gets busy? If you are like most people, this happens a lot. It may be a goal around your health, your relationships, your work, your income — it doesn't matter what part of life it is in or how bad you say you want it.

When you have no one checking in with your progress and how you are doing, it is easy to let that goal fade to the background. This is especially true if the goal is lofty or something you aren't sure you can achieve.

Chapter 10

Not only does a coach keep you accountable, a coach also provides expert advice from someone who knows the next steps. The feedback is real and constructive, not theoretical or general. You won't be told that you don't matter or to get over those things that are bothering you.

For example, I worked with another young hairdresser who was experiencing what I would term as extreme bullying in the workplace. I experienced this exact same scenario when I was a young hairdresser and didn't have the skills to deal with the issues. I knew exactly how she felt – how sad, frustrated and angry she was at her coworkers who absolutely should have known better. She was constantly excluded from conversations as well as outside activities and made to feel as if there was no place for her in that salon.

I knew from my own experience the real issue was the fact that she was smart, liked by clients and a great hairdresser, despite being so young. Her co-workers were jealous of her! She needed the support of someone who wouldn't just say to ignore them. That is not a good solution at all, and I knew it. She needed the skills to understand what was going on to conquer that environment.

A lot of what I did with this client was build up her self-esteem, which had been largely crushed by the words and actions contained in this toxic work environment. She came through that storm with some great people skills and now works for herself. The experience and stress she endured made her a much stronger person because she found a way to move on to something better – a fabulous outcome, in my opinion.

A coach or mentor can get you through that kind of tough spot and teach you how to handle yourself should it recur. But that is not the only thing I do. As I told you, I also owned a salon, and a large part of my business is working with salon owners on their biggest issue, which is, as you may have guessed, people. Usually, this means staff. I know from experience that the majority of issues that a salon owner deals with have nothing to do with clients, but everything to do with the salon staff not getting along.

It is quite common that I will do a seminar or onsite training to teach staff members how to work together again after a blowup. I recently worked with an organization that was experiencing significant bullying in the workplace. This wasn't a staff of young hairdressers, as one might expect, but a fully experienced staff who were all in their forties and fifties.

You might assume that by this age, they would have a better interpersonal skill set, but that's not always true. If a person never endeavors to improve their communication skills, then they will never get better at it, no matter their age. In this case, they hadn't gotten better; they had gotten worse, even though they had worked alongside each other every day for years.

The owner asked for my emotional intelligence program, and I worked with the group to give them the support to understand how to communicate and understand differences in communication styles as well as the skills to move forward. This was a tough group because, as with many groups of people who spend a great deal of time together, they had some hard-core ingrained habits that had to be addressed. They were very mean to one another

Chapter 10

out of habit and had to put in the work to level up to a professional work environment.

The most intelligent and successful people I have ever been around have all had coaches. They see the value in being able to shortcut their way to success. They also see no value in struggling to learn every skill through trial and error. The amount of time and money wasted doing that can be immense. They know that asking for and seeking out quality help gets them to where they want to be faster and easier than going it alone.

My Desire for You

I created this book, companion workbook and gratitude journal with you in mind. I wanted a way for you to uncover truths about your authentic self and make decisions about what you want for your life. The idea is that it will start you on your journey to get you to that next level in your life and beyond. I created the very thing I wish I'd had all those years ago, as I believe it would have improved my journey immensely.

Being able to understand yourself without all the emotional clutter and noise is the only way to get clear on what you can be. Out in the world, we are a different version of ourselves. But when we are alone in the quiet of our mind is when we go deep and understand that life has an expiration date. None of us know how much time we have, yet so many of us know there is more out there for us to achieve.

One desire I have for you is that you listen to that voice and nurture the small flame within your soul that desires more. There is no such thing as 'stuck' in life unless you refuse to take hold of the power you have to change.

Now is your time to take hold of the knowledge being offered and make your life one that you will someday look back on, amazed at your progress and at the incredible person you have become.

About the Author

Donna Piromalli has empowered individuals to achieve new heights in wealth, success and happiness through her books, coaching programs and speaking events. She is also the founder of The Counselling, Mediation & Relationship Centre, a company providing programs, seminars and sessions for both individuals and businesses that help their goals become reality.

After more than 25 years in the hairdressing industry as both a salon owner and instructor, Donna is now a registered and accredited counsellor and mediator working in her own private practice. She has years of experience working with individuals, couples, families and businesses.

Donna specialises in Relationship Training and Conflict Resolution for both families and business. She also supports individual clients with depression, anxiety, trauma, panic attacks, PTSD, separation & divorce, parenting training, grief & loss, self-esteem improvement, as well as bullying and anger management issues.

As a registered Family Dispute Resolution Practitioner (FDRP) with the Attorney General's Office, Donna can issue Section 60(I) certificates pursuant to the provisions of the Family Law Act 1975, when mediation is not appropriate, enabling the parties' access to the court process.

Donna is also a Child Consultant, as child inclusive practice engages children and brings their voice forward to the mediation session. She works with and supports children, to discover their needs during the separation and divorce process.

Donna's mission is to help people become empowered leaders in all aspects of their personal and professional lives.

www.DonnaPiromalli.com

www.ingramcontent.com/pod-product-compliance
Lightning Source LLC
Chambersburg PA
CBHW070101080526
44586CB00013B/1142